Angel Reiki

*Discover the power of universal energy
and the guidance of the angels to transform your life*

Isis Estrada

Holos Arts Project

Publisher: Holos Arts Project

All rights reserved - Copyright ©2023 Isis Estrada

Editor's Note: All rights of this book are reserved. No part may be used or reproduced by any means, graphic, electronic or mechanical, including photocopying, recording, or by any information storage retrieval system without the written permission of the author, except in the case of brief quotations included in articles and critical reviews.

The purpose of this book is to present an alternative therapeutic method, which in no way should replace a medical treatment or prescribed medicine. The topics covered here are an auxiliary to any type of medical therapy and are presented as a complementary option.

Angel REIKI
Isis Estrada

Holos Arts Project

CONTENTS

Preliminary Words 07
Introduction to Reiki 09
History of Reiki 11
How Reiki works 13
Introduction to Angels 15
Different types of Angels 17
The Archangels 21
Archangels and symbols of Reiki 26
Selecting the Angels who will assist you 31
What can you ask of Angels? 37
Communication with the Angels 39
How to keep a diary of messages from the Angels . . . 41
Preparation for a Reiki session with Angels 43
A complete Reiki self-healing session with Angels . . . 45
A complete Reiki session with Angels to heal others . . . 48
A complete Reiki session with Crystals and help from the Angels . . 51
Practice: How to make a grid of Crystals, Angels and Reiki . . 54
Guided Meditation: Distance Healing with Angels . . . 57
Spiritual protection with the divine help of the Angels . . 59
Procedure to clean your house of negativity, with the help of the Angels. . 61
Cleansing the Aura and Chakra Blockages 63
Guided meditation to heal emotional wounds, with the help of the Angels 65
Guided meditation with Angels to manifest the law of attraction . 68
How to become a certified Reiki practitioner with Angels . . 71
Preparing for Attunement 72
Reiki attunement with Angels 73
Conclusions 76

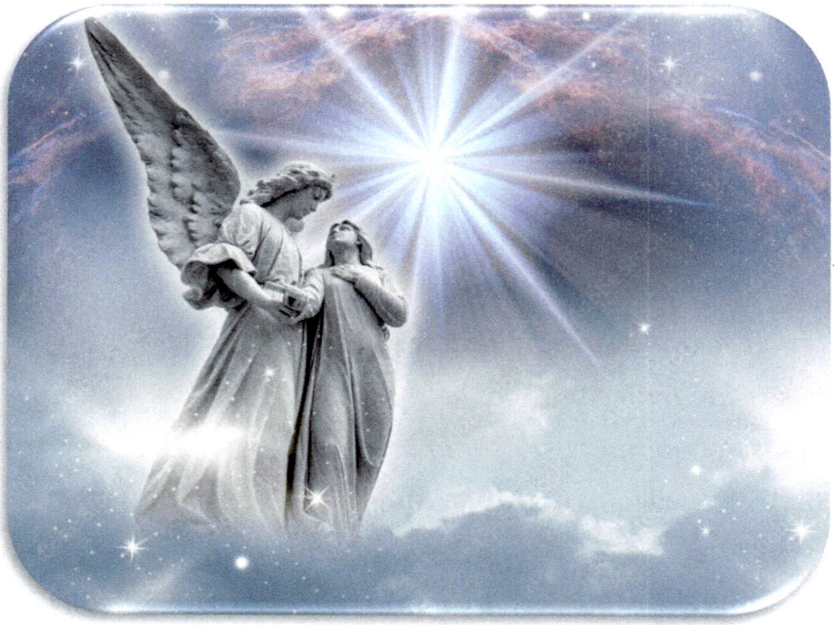

Preliminary Words

The healing energies of Reiki, along with the help of divine holy angels, are a heavenly gift available to support you in all areas of your existence. These vibrations are clean and potent, and can offer you unparalleled assistance on your journey, whether you are facing difficulties, seeking direction, or in need of healing in any aspect, physical, emotional or spiritual.

To receive the support of these benevolent angels, you need only open your heart to them and allow their love and guidance to flow into your life. This book provides you with a clear and easy-to-follow path to receive this divine assistance. With step-by-step instructions and detailed guides, you will discover in its pages a treasure trove of wisdom and knowledge designed especially for you.

I am very happy that you have chosen to learn this method of Reiki energy that I have taught to many students over many years in face-to-face classes. During this time, I have observed that Reiki and angels seem to complement each other in an extraordinary way.

In this text designed as a course, you will learn the technique to use the healing energy of Reiki in combination with the wisdom and power of angels to transform your life and the lives of others.

You will explore the fascinating world of angels, learn about the different hierarchies that exist among them, and discover the deep connection they have with Reiki. You will learn about the archangels and their symbols specific to Reiki, as well as the guardian angels and other spiritual beings that can assist you in your Reiki practice.

Through practical exercises and guided meditations, you will learn to communicate with the angels and archangels, and how to invoke their help in your Reiki sessions. You will discover methods to cleanse the human aura and Chakras with the assistance of the angels, and how to perform complete Reiki sessions for yourself and others, including distance sessions.

In addition, you will learn advanced techniques such as how to clear areas of negativity with the help of angels, and the steps to create a crystal Reiki grid to request the assistance of your angels for your purposes and goals. You will also receive advice to open your own angel Reiki therapist practice, if you wish. Also, a special attunement is included to connect you more efficiently with Reiki energy and amplify your ability to work with it.

This book is a course in the full extent of the word, which follows the world standards of the subject, and is accredited by The International Guild of Complementary Therapists (IGCT), from England. Anyone who has completed the course can request their diploma of completion, personalized with name and date, which is issued by the Center for Alternative Therapies "Mystic Path", in Mexico City, of which I am the general director.

In the last section of the book, I give more extensive explanations of the way to request the attunement and diploma.

No matter what stage of your journey you are in, whether you feel disoriented, confused, hurt or in need of strength, the holy angels are there to be with you and guide you. Their love is unconditional and their power has no limits. You just need to open your heart, trust and allow their help to flow into your life. Remember that you are surrounded by divine love and that the angels are always by your side, ready to assist you at all times.

Introduction to Reiki

Reiki is an ancient healing practice that has gained popularity around the world due to its benefits to the mind, body and spirit. Originating in Japan, Reiki is based on the idea that we all possess a universal life energy that flows through us. When this energy becomes unbalanced or blocked, illness and discomfort can occur. Reiki focuses on restoring balance and harmony to this energy, promoting healing and wellness.

The word "Reiki" comes from two Japanese terms: "Rei", which means "universal energy", and "Ki", which refers to the "vital energy" that flows in every living being. Reiki is based on the idea that practitioners can channel this energy through their hands and transfer it to other people or themselves to promote healing and deep relaxation.

The system of Reiki was developed in the early twentieth century (specifically, from 1922), by Dr. Mikao Usui, a Japanese spiritual master, who was looking for a form of healing that could be accessible and applied by anyone. Usui drew on ancient Eastern healing techniques and undertook a meditation and fasting retreat on Mount Kurama, where he received a spiritual revelation that gave him the symbols and techniques of Reiki. From that moment on, he began to teach and spread this practice throughout Japan.

Reiki is based on the idea that we all have the ability to channel universal energy through our hands. During a Reiki session, the practitioner gently places his or her hands on different parts of the recipient's body, following a series of specific positions. The hands can also be a few centimeters away from the body, if the patient does not want physical contact. Through these positions, energy is allowed to flow and be distributed in a balanced way, eliminating blockages and promoting healing on all levels: physical, mental, emotional and spiritual. Reiki is not linked to any specific religion and can be practiced independently of individual beliefs.

One of the most outstanding aspects of Reiki is its ability to reduce stress and promote a deep sense of relaxation. Many people experience a feeling of peace and calm during Reiki sessions, which helps them release tension and facilitate the healing process. In addition, Reiki can complement and enhance other medical treatments and therapies, as it has no negative side effects and can be used in conjunction with any other health care approach.

Reiki is not only limited to individual therapy sessions with a patient but can also be applied autonomously through self-healing. Reiki practitioners learn techniques to channel universal energy to themselves, balancing their own energy system and promoting their personal well-being. This practice can be especially beneficial in reducing daily stress, increasing vitality and maintaining a state of overall harmony.

One of the unique characteristics of Reiki is that it is transmitted through initiation or attunement by a Reiki master to his or her disciple. During this process, the practitioner's energy channel is opened and expanded, allowing him or her to access higher levels of channeling and awareness. The attunement also establishes a special connection with the universal energy source, allowing the practitioner to become a Reiki channel for life.

Reiki is a holistic healing practice that uses universal energy to promote balance and well-being on all levels. Through its gentle, non-invasive approach, Reiki can help relieve stress, reduce discomfort and promote an overall sense of calm and relaxation.

The practice of Reiki has spread throughout the world and has been integrated into various settings, such as hospitals, clinics, wellness centers and personal settings. Many people have experienced the benefits of Reiki in their daily lives, whether to alleviate physical ailments, or to foster greater emotional balance.

Whether receiving a Reiki session or practicing it on oneself, this ancient technique offers a path to healing and self-transformation.

History of Reiki

The history of Reiki dates back to the beginning of the 20th century in Japan, with its founder, Dr. Mikao Usui as the central figure. Usui, born on August 15, 1865 in the Taniai district, was a man of great spirituality and curiosity in the field of healing. His search for answers led him to develop a system of energy therapy known today as Reiki.

The key moment in the history of Reiki occurred in 1922, when Mikao Usui undertook a meditation and fasting retreat on Mount Kurama. During his 21-day retreat, Usui experienced a spiritual revelation that transformed his life and laid the foundation for Reiki. According to legend, while meditating under a waterfall, he received a powerful healing energy that gave him the symbols and techniques of Reiki.

After his experience on Mount Kurama, Usui began practicing and teaching Reiki in the city of Kyoto. He established a healing clinic called Usui Reiki Ryoho Gakkai, where he treated numerous patients and trained others in this healing technique. As his reputation grew, Usui traveled throughout Japan spreading Reiki and teaching new practitioners.

One of Usui's most prominent students was Chujiro Hayashi, an officer in the Imperial Japanese Navy. Hayashi expanded and systematized Usui's system, introducing new techniques and practices, and establishing the three levels of Reiki training: Reiki I, Reiki II and Reiki III (also known as mastery). Hayashi also adapted Reiki to treat specific conditions, developing different protocols and hand positions.

After Mikao Usui's death in 1926, Chujiro Hayashi continued to spread Reiki and train new teachers. One of his most notable students was Hawayo Takata, a woman of Hawaiian origin who traveled to Japan in search of healing. Takata received treatment from Hayashi and was so impressed with the results that she decided to study and become a Reiki master.

Hawayo Takata brought Reiki to the West in the mid-20th century and became the main disseminator of this technique in the United States and Canada. During his time in the West, Takata made important adaptations to Hayashi's system and laid the foundation for the global expansion of Reiki. She trained numerous Western masters, who in turn passed the practice on to others, helping to establish Reiki as a popular form of healing throughout the world.

Over the decades, Reiki has evolved and branched out into different currents and approaches. Variants such as Tibetan Usui Reiki, Karuna Reiki and Kundalini Reiki, among others, have been developed. However, all are based on the fundamental principles of the original system established by Mikao Usui and expanded by his successors.

In summary, the history of Reiki originates with Mikao Usui in Japan in the early 20th century. Through the teachings and legacy of Usui, as well as his successors such as Chujiro Hayashi and Hawayo Takata, Reiki has been transmitted and spread worldwide. Today, Reiki is recognized as an energetic healing practice that promotes balance and well-being in body, mind and spirit.

How Reiki works

According to the Usui Ryoho tradition, and to the experience of many years of several masters and practitioners around the world, it can be affirmed that Reiki:

* It is an energy that tends to bring stabilization to living organisms, places and situations; which translates in terms of health, harmony and protection.

* It is a positive flow, that is, it is only accessed when it is used for the benefit of oneself, others, and without selfish purposes. When the motivation is malevolent or materialistic, it simply blocks the flow of Reiki.

* Reiki is accessed voluntarily. That is, when the person does not wish to be healed or benefit from Reiki, there is a barrier between the individual and the Reiki healer's energy current.

* Reiki exists and flows everywhere. The healer, the only thing he/she does is to become an enhancer and channeler of this energy, consciously directing it towards what he/she wishes to heal. The healer is not the one who heals... it is Reiki who does it.

* Reiki is an intelligent energy that finds its own ways of healing. It is free. We humans intuit that we can use it, however, our Chakras function poorly due to our negative emotions and materialistic attachments. The way to be able to channel Reiki energy is only after an attunement, to initiate its activation with the universal flow of life.

* It has been demonstrated that attunement can only be transmitted from person to person; that is, from teacher to student.

* Absolutely everyone has the potential ability to access Reiki.

* Reiki is considered a complementary therapy. It should never replace a conventional medical treatment. Any type of energetic therapy is a support and contributes to a faster improvement of the person.

As mentioned, the vital energy of the universe is everywhere. It is a creative and regenerative energy. Like an invisible fabric, it gives cohesion to the universe, permeates everything, including ourselves.

When using Reiki, we consciously potentiate that energy, we channel it to our Chakras, to activate them and thus benefit at all levels of being, of its healing energy. We can heal ourselves and, after having gone through an attunement ritual, we function as channelers of that energy to direct it to other beings.

After manifesting the intention to channel the energy, Reiki begins to flow to the healer, to enter from his seventh Chakra, the crown Chakra, and permeates the other 6 Chakras, activating them gradually, in a constant flow. For the transmission of Reiki, it branches from the throat Chakra to the hands, so that the healer can radiate the energy for healing through them. In a later chapter of this book, we will discuss the Chakras in more detail.

It is important to mention that the awakening of the Chakras will not happen all at once, not even after an attunement. If it were sudden, it would produce a lack of control. It is a gradual process. The awakening of the Chakras occurs little by little, to give the individual a chance to get used to and master the Reiki energy that is being activated in his or her being.

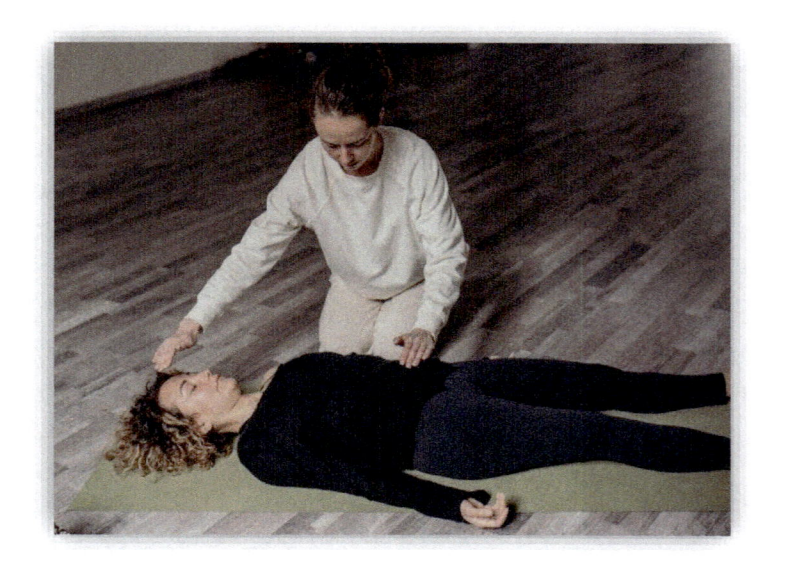

Introduction to Angels

The spiritual beings known as angels transcend religious and cultural boundaries. Although they are often associated primarily with Christianity, their importance also encompasses other faiths such as Judaism, Islam, voodoo and indigenous religions in Africa, as well as some Eastern religions. This implies that angels are inclusive and are not exclusively linked to a single religion. As spiritual beings, they are part of diverse belief systems and are willing to provide help, regardless of people's religious affiliation or lack thereof.

It is relevant to note that angels are recognized as message bearers and guardians, without exercising control or dominion over human beings, nor vice versa. They are spiritual entities willing to provide help when requested, but they always respect our freedom of choice. This implies that angels will never attempt to alter our decisions or actions but are present to provide guidance and support in our paths.

It is fascinating to observe how angels, as a spiritual entity, transcend temporal and spatial limitations. They are considered multidimensional beings with the ability to coexist in different places and times simultaneously. For example, one may request the help of Archangel Michael, and at the same time he may be assisting someone in a distant location. This amazing quality implies that angels are not subject to restrictions of location or time in offering their support, which is a difficult concept to conceive of from our human perspective. Nevertheless, this notion is a belief rooted in numerous spiritual traditions, adding an interesting nuance to the understanding of these spiritual entities.

It is of utmost importance to note that angels are characterized by their benevolent nature. In no case do they possess the capacity to inflict harm on anyone. Their fundamental purpose is to offer us support and guidance in our journey through life, with no intention of causing harm or interfering with our free will. Therefore, when we turn to them for help, we can be certain that their assistance will always be positive and to our benefit. It is comforting to know that their presence is motivated by a sincere desire to contribute to our well-being and personal development. This conviction gives us the confidence to open our hearts to their positive influence in our lives.

It is important to emphasize that the relationship with angels does not imply absolute reverence. It is not a matter of worshipping them as divine entities, but rather of establishing a communicative and spiritual bond with them. Angels are conceived as creations of divinity, destined to transmit messages and provide support to human beings on their spiritual path. Consequently, interaction with angels is based on a relationship founded on respect and gratitude, in which their help and guidance is requested in times of need. This approach is characterized by a deeper and more empathic understanding, in which angels are recognized as loving servants, willing to assist us in our spiritual growth without demanding absolute devotion.

Therefore, angels represent spiritual entities that transcend the boundaries of diverse beliefs and cultures, always being ready to offer their help when requested. These beings are recognized as message bearers and protectors, without exercising control over human beings or being subdued by them and stand out for their ability to overcome temporal and spatial limitations. Their benevolent nature excludes them from causing harm, and the relationship with them is built on spiritual communication and connection, where they are asked for help and guidance with respect and gratitude. This approach fosters a warm and understanding interaction, where angels are seen as spiritual allies willing to accompany us on our life journey.

Different types of Angels

There are 9 levels of angels: Seraphim, Cherubim, Thrones, Dominations, Virtues, Powers, Principalities, Archangels and Guardian Angels.

The 1st Triad resides in the highest realm of heaven:

Seraphim occupy the closest position to divinity, being beings of pure light and representing the highest level within the angelic hierarchy. Their name, which means "those who burn", symbolizes the divine love and wisdom they emanate. In their continuous praise of God, they chant the sacred song "Holy, holy, holy" to convey the divine glory. These angelic beings are endowed with six pairs of wings, two of which guard their feet as a sign of humility, two others protect their purity by covering their chests, while the remaining two conceal their radiant radiance by covering their faces. Within their function, the Seraphim assume the role of purifying other angels and also human beings by means of their sacred fire. This spiritual fire symbolizes the transformation and purification of the soul, encouraging elevation towards greater closeness with the divine. Their work transcends the celestial sphere, directly impacting the spirituality of those they guide and purify.

The Cherubim, located on the second highest rung of the angelic hierarchy, personify pure love and their name, which means "those who pray", highlights their role as guardians of divine wisdom and the stars. These angelic beings are distinguished by possessing two pairs of wings, as well as four distinctive faces: the first is the countenance of a lion, representing wild animals; the second is the face of an ox, symbolizing domesticated animals; the third corresponds to a human being, encapsulating all humanity; and the fourth is the face of an eagle, encompassing the representation of all birds. As special guardians, the Cherubim have the responsibility of guarding the throne of God and the tree of life in paradise, thus symbolizing their role as protectors of the divine essences and the primordial source of life. In addition, they are attributed the function of messengers in charge of transmitting prophetic visions and sacred knowledge through communication between heaven and earth.

The Thrones play a crucial role in acting as the bridge connecting heaven with our world, and are entrusted with overseeing fairness and justice on behalf of God. Their appellation, meaning "those who uphold," reflects their role as bearers of divine will and cosmic laws. These angelic beings exhibit a singular appearance: they take the form of wheels covered with eyes and wings, which gives them an impressive and mysterious image. In addition, their movement is characterized by speed and harmony, which denotes a precise and coordinated execution of their functions.

The Thrones assume the important responsibility of maintaining order and balance in the vast universe, also inspiring rulers and judges on earth to act with justice and righteousness in their roles. This connection between heaven and our world allows them to exert a beneficial influence on the earthly plane.

The 2nd Triad is located between the Earth and the sky:

The Dominations exercise a function of management and direction over the angels, always fulfilling the will of God. Their designation, which means "those who rule", confers on them the role of leaders among the angels of lower hierarchies. In their appearance, they are more similar to the image we usually associate with angels: they are human-shaped, winged, and carry a sword or a scepter in their hands. These angelic beings play a crucial role in regulating the flow of divine grace, thus maintaining order and harmony on the celestial plane. They also play a role as messengers of miracles and blessings destined for humanity, which enhances their beneficial role in people's lives. The Dominations, acting as leaders and coordinators of the lower angels, play an essential role in the execution of the divine will in the spiritual and earthly world. Their work of management and regulation contributes to the maintenance of balance and harmony in the cosmos, projecting an image of order and purpose in the divine plan.

The Virtues exercise dominion over the sun, the moon, the stars and all the planets, and their name, which means "those who give strength", reflects their responsibility to maintain balance and harmony in nature. These angelic beings take on the appearance of rays of light, wearing a crown of flowers on their heads, giving them an image of beauty and splendor. Their crucial role is to bestow gifts and miracles to human beings, giving them strength to overcome difficulties and temptations in their lives. Likewise, the Virtues assume the role of protectors of travelers and pilgrims, offering guidance and assistance in their journeys.

The Powers, as peaceful warriors, play an essential role in purifying the lower energies on the earthly plane. Their name, meaning "those who have power," emphasizes their role as defenders of justice and truth. They are entrusted with the important task of confronting and neutralizing negative energy, as well as protecting the divine order from negative entities that attempt to disrupt it. Their appearance resembles that of armored soldiers, holding a sword or spear in their hands, symbolizing their readiness and willingness to face spiritual challenges. The Powers play a crucial role in protecting human beings from spiritual attacks, strengthening their faith and will in times of adversity. They are also guardians of history and collective memory, protecting the knowledge and teachings that have shaped humanity throughout time. Their work as purifiers and guardians contributes to the maintenance of balance and harmony on the earthly plane, creating an environment conducive to spiritual development and collective well-being.

The 3rd Triad is closer to Earth:

The Principalities assume a watchdog role over the Earth, playing a leading role in promoting peace. Their designation, meaning "those who preside," reflects their responsibility to guide leaders and nations in the pursuit of harmony and collective well-being. Sometimes we identify them with the angels present during the Christmas season, and they are entrusted with the important task of assisting in violent situations, such as wars or conflicts, seeking to mitigate their impact and promote peaceful solutions. Frequently, the Principalities are represented carrying scepters and crowns, symbols of their authority and dignity in their role as guides and preservers of the divine order. In addition to their work with human beings, these angels play a relevant role as protectors of nature and animals, promoting respect and harmony in the interaction between humanity and the natural environment.

The Archangels have a supervisory role over both human beings and guardian angels. Each represents a distinctive aspect of God and has a specific mission on the divine plane. These angelic beings are present to assist us and will play a prominent role in the content of this class. Tradition points to the existence of seven main Archangels, namely: Michael, recognized as the warrior of faith; Gabriel, considered the messenger of hope; Uriel, bearer of light; Ariel, protector of nature; Camuel, healer of love; Jophiel, teacher of wisdom; and Zadkiel, dispenser of forgiveness. Information about these Archangels is recorded in sacred texts of Christianity and Judaism, such as the Book of Revelation and the Book of Enoch. These writings are of special importance in the study of angelology and offer us a detailed perspective on the roles and attributes of these spiritual beings.

Guardian Angels are angelic beings personally assigned to each individual throughout his or her life. Each person is born with two of these angels and, throughout his or her existence, may gain or lose their companionship depending on individual circumstances and needs. These Guardian Angels accompany the person from the moment of conception until their last breath, assisting them in the realization of their divine purpose. Their essential function is to protect, guide, comfort and inspire the person to whom they are assigned. In this way, Guardian Angels become loyal friends and spiritual allies, providing constant support throughout the life journey.

Communication with these celestial beings can be established through various means, such as prayer, meditation or intuition, allowing for a deep and meaningful connection with them. This special relationship with Guardian Angels can bring a sense of protection and spiritual companionship that positively influences people's lives.

There are angels to help us with everything: abundance, well-being, romance, health, emotions, everything. So remember that no matter what situation you are in, there are angels everywhere. They are God's messengers and they are ready to help you at any time. You just have to ask for their assistance and be attentive to their signs. Angels can manifest themselves in various ways: finding feathers, unexpected coins, repeating numbers, mystical dreams, synchronicities, etc. Angels love you unconditionally and want the best for you. Trust them and let their light guide you.

The Archangels

In the vast spiritual realm, archangels are presented as beings of light and wisdom, ready to guide and protect humanity on its earthly journey. These powerful angelic entities have been recognized and worshipped throughout history by various spiritual traditions and religions. In this chapter, we will explore the main archangels and their characteristics, providing a comprehensive view of these magnificent spiritual figures.

1. Archangel Michael: The Celestial Warrior

The archangel Michael is undoubtedly one of the best known and most revered archangels in different cultures. His name, which means "Who is like God?", reflects his unwavering devotion to the Creator and his role as leader of the heavenly armies. He is recognized as the protector and defender against negative forces and destructive energies. Michael exudes a courageous and powerful energy, often depicted with a sword and shield, symbolizing his strength and protection.

When we connect with the archangel Michael, he invites us to find the courage to face challenges and overcome obstacles. His courageous presence infuses us with a sense of security and confidence in times of adversity.

2. Archangel Raphael: The Divine Healer

Archangel Raphael is known as the divine healer, the one who brings comfort and restoration to bodies, minds and souls. His name means "God heals," and his healing energy extends to all who invoke him. He is often depicted with a staff, a symbol of guidance and support in the healing process.

When we seek Raphael's assistance, this loving archangel helps us to heal physical and emotional wounds. He inspires us to find harmony and balance in our lives and guides us toward wellness in all aspects of our being.

3. Archangel Gabriel: The Messenger of Truth

The archangel Gabriel is the heavenly messenger, known for delivering divine news and revelations. His name means "God is my strength", and his presence radiates purity and wisdom. He is commonly depicted carrying a trumpet, symbolizing his role as herald of the divine will.

When we invoke Gabriel, he helps us to open ourselves to truth and clarity. His guidance encourages us to communicate with honesty and compassion and inspires us to listen and understand the messages coming from the spiritual plane.

4. Archangel Uriel: Guardian of Wisdom

The archangel Uriel is the guardian of wisdom and enlightenment. His name means "God is my light," and his presence shines with a calming and enlightening energy. He is often depicted holding a scroll, which represents divine knowledge.

By invoking Uriel, he opens the way to inner wisdom and helps us find answers in times of confusion. His light guides us to deeper understanding and invites us to see the beauty and wisdom that resides in every aspect of existence.

5. Archangel Metatron: The Guardian of the Children

The archangel Metatron is known as the guardian of children and newborn souls. His name means "beyond the throne," reflecting his proximity to the Creator. Metatron is said to have been a human being who ascended to angelic form and became the archangel he is today.

Metatron guides and protects children, offering them wisdom and love during their earthly journey. His presence helps us to connect with our inner childhood and to maintain a pure and open heart in our daily lives.

6. Archangel Chamuel: The Seeker of Love

The archangel Chamuel, whose name means "the one who seeks God," is the archangel of love and compassion. His energy focuses on helping us find love within ourselves and in our relationships with others. Chamuel is often depicted holding a pink flame, symbolizing unconditional love.

By connecting with Chamuel, he helps us to overcome conflicts and find peace in our relationships. He also guides us in the search for self-love and teaches us to love and accept ourselves as we are.

7. Archangel Jophiel: The Illuminator of Knowledge

The archangel Jophiel is known as the illuminator of divine knowledge and wisdom. His name means "beauty of God," and his presence radiates a golden light that helps us to see the beauty and harmony in all things. Jophiel is presented as a guide on the path of learning and spiritual growth.

By invoking Jophiel, he helps us to find inspiration and creativity in our lives. He teaches us to appreciate the beauty that surrounds us and to recognize the divinity in every aspect of existence.

Archangels are beings of light and love who offer us guidance and protection on our spiritual path. Each one of them possesses unique characteristics that we can invoke to receive their assistance in different aspects of our lives. By connecting with these powerful beings, we open ourselves to an inexhaustible source of wisdom, healing, love and protection that accompanies us on every step of our earthly journey.

Archangels and Symbols of Reiki

In this chapter, we will explore the connection between the archangels and the Reiki symbols, two fundamental elements for the practice of this energy therapy.

As we have explained in the previous chapter, the archangels are the angels of the highest rank and power, who act as messengers and guardians of God. Each of them has a specific mission and a distinguishing quality. The archangels assist us in all aspects of our lives, as long as we invoke them with love and respect. They do not belong to any religion or creed but are at the service of all humanity.

Reiki is a natural healing technique that uses the laying on of hands to transmit the vital energy of the universe. Reiki is based on the principle that everything is composed of energy, and that when this energy flows freely, balance and harmony is produced in the body, mind and spirit.

Reiki symbols are signs that represent different aspects and functions of Reiki energy. The symbols are activated by mental intention and visualization, plus they allow the energy to be focused for specific purposes. Reiki symbols act as keys that open access to a higher form of energy. Each symbol has its own vibration and meaning.

We will use five main Reiki symbols:

- Cho Ku Rei: the symbol of power. It is used to increase or decrease the intensity of Reiki energy, as needed. It is also used to protect, cleanse and purify people, places or objects. Its shape is reminiscent of a spiral or a ray, and its color is white or silver.

- Sei He Ki: the mental-emotional symbol. It is used to balance and harmonize emotions and thoughts, as well as to release blockages, traumas and addictions. It also favors communication, creativity and intuition. Its shape is reminiscent of a wave or a snake, and its color is blue or violet.

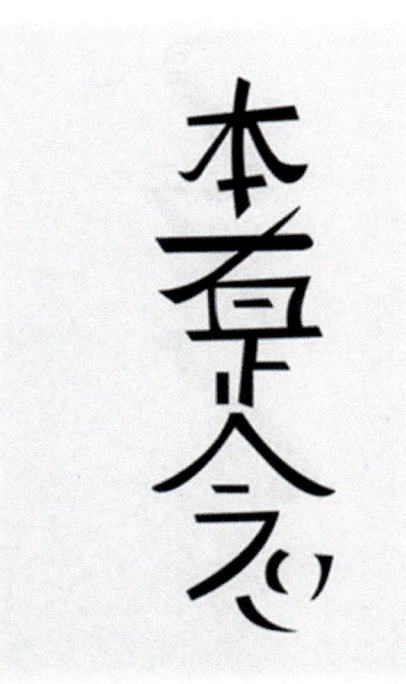

- Hon Sha Ze Sho Nen: the symbol of distance. It is used to send Reiki energy through space and time, regardless of physical or temporal limitations. It also serves to connect with life purpose, karma and past lives. Its shape is reminiscent of a temple or torch, and its color is gold or orange.

- Dai Ko Myo: the master symbol. It is used to access the highest level of Reiki energy, which implies enlightenment and connection with the divine source. It is also used to initiate others into Reiki, and to heal the soul and spirit. Its shape is reminiscent of a sun or a flower, and its color is violet or white.

- Raku: the symbol of harmony. It is used to seal and end a Reiki session, ensuring that the energy is well distributed and balanced. It is also used to cut energetic ties that are no longer beneficial, and to facilitate the attunement process. Its shape is reminiscent of a lightning bolt or feather, and its color is black or red.

Now, how do the archangels relate to the Reiki symbols? The answer is that each archangel has an affinity with one or more Reiki symbols, depending on their mission and vibration. By invoking an archangel while using a Reiki symbol, we enhance the effect of both elements, creating a synergy of light and love.

Here is a list of the best known archangels and the Reiki symbols associated with them:

- Michael: the archangel of protection, justice and truth. His name means "who is like God". His color is blue or purple. He is associated with the symbol Cho Ku Rei, as both have a power of cleansing and defense. It is also associated with the symbol Dai Ko Myo, as both have a power of enlightenment and connection with divinity.

- Raphael: the archangel of healing, love and grace. His name means "God heals". His color is green or pink. He is associated with the symbol Sei He Ki, as both have a power of balance and emotional harmony. It is also associated with the symbol Hon Sha Ze Sho Nen, as both have a power of distant healing and connection with karma.

- Gabriel: the archangel of communication, creativity and conception. His name means "God is my strength". His color is white or silver. He is associated with the symbol Sei He Ki, as both have a power of expression and mental clarity. It is also associated with the symbol Raku, as both have a power to seal and finalize processes.

- Uriel: the archangel of wisdom, transformation and transmutation. His name means "the light of God". His color is gold or orange. He is associated with the symbol Hon Sha Ze Sho Nen, as both have a power of connection with life purpose and past lives. It is also associated with the symbol Dai Ko Myo, as both have a power of illumination and connection with the divine source.

- Chamuel: the archangel of unconditional love, compassion and peace. His name means "the one who sees God". His color is pink or green. He is associated with the symbol Sei He Ki, as both have a power of balance and emotional harmony. It is also associated with the symbol Cho Ku Rei, as both have a power of protection and purification.

- Jophiel: the archangel of beauty, joy and gratitude. His name means "the beauty of God". His color is yellow or golden. He is associated with the symbol Hon Sha Ze Sho Nen, as both have a power of connection with life purpose and past lives. It is also associated with the symbol Cho Ku Rei, as both have a power of cleansing and purification.

- Zadquiel: the archangel of forgiveness, mercy and deliverance. His name means "the justice of God". His color is violet or indigo. He is associated with the symbol Dai Ko Myo, as both have a power of illumination and connection with the divine source. It is also associated with the symbol Raku, as both have a power to cut energetic ties that are no longer beneficial.

These are just a few examples of how you can combine the archangels and Reiki symbols to create a deeper and more enriching experience. I encourage you to experiment for yourself with the different possibilities and find the ones that best suit your needs and preferences.

Remember that the archangels and Reiki symbols are tools available to everyone, which only require your sincere intention and your openness to love. There is no right or wrong way to use them, only a personal and intuitive way.

Selecting the Angels who will assist you

In this chapter, we will explore how you can choose those celestial beings who will accompany you on your path to wellness and spiritual evolution. Angels are beings of light that guide, protect and support us in our challenges and life purposes. Through Reiki and a conscious connection with them, we can experience a loving and healing presence that encourages us to reach our full potential.

It is crucial to remember that there is no wrong choice in selecting an angel to work with you. Every angel is willing to give you unconditional help and love, regardless of your specific circumstances or needs. However, by attuning to the energy of a particular angel, you can receive more specific and profound guidance in certain areas of your life. Below, I will offer you a simple process for determining which angel might be best suited to accompany you on your quest.

1. Reflect on your needs and desires:

Before connecting with the angels, take a moment to reflect on your life and the areas in which you seek support and guidance. Ask yourself what aspects of your existence require the most attention or what you wish to achieve in your life. Some common areas include health, relationships, prosperity, spiritual wisdom, protection or self-esteem. Observe your emotions and feelings; they will indicate what are the most pressing needs in your life at this time.

2. Investigate the angels associated with your needs.

Once you have identified your needs and desires, research the angels who are connected to those specific areas. In the angelic tradition, it is believed that there are angels who are especially connected to certain aspects of human life. Explore their attributes and qualities to determine which of them might be most attuned to your current needs.

3. Meditation.

Once you have chosen an angel or even several angels that catch your attention, it is time to connect with them through meditation. Find a quiet place where you can sit or lie down comfortably. Close your eyes, breathe deeply and relax. Visualize a bright white light surrounding you, protecting you and filling you with love and peace. With a calm mind, direct your thoughts to the angel you have chosen. Call upon their loving presence and ask for their guidance and assistance in your specific needs and desires. Remain in this meditative state for a few minutes, allowing the angel's energy to mingle with you and bring you the clarity you seek.

4. Pay attention to the signs.

Once you have established this connection with the angel, keep an open mind and pay attention to the signs that may appear in your daily life. Angels often communicate with us through synchronicities, inspirational thoughts, vivid dreams or intuitive sensations. Being receptive to these signals will allow you to receive the guidance and support the angel has to offer.

5. Trust your intuition.

The process of choosing an angel can be very personal, and it is essential that you trust your intuition during this process. If you feel a deep and comforting connection with a particular angel, follow that inner guidance. The heart always knows what is best for you. Remember that all angels are willing to help you, and there is no wrong choice.

6. Work with several angels if necessary.

Don't feel limited to working with only one angel. You can establish connections with several angels according to your changing needs. Some situations may require the guidance of one specific angel, while other circumstances may benefit from the combined influence of several angels.

Remember that angels always respect your free will and will only intervene when asked for their help. Do not hesitate to invoke them and ask for their guidance at any time.

The process of choosing the angels who will help you is an act of love and self-knowledge. By reflecting on your needs and desires, researching the angels associated with them, meditating and attuning to their energy, and trusting your intuition, you can establish a meaningful connection with these celestial beings. They will offer you their unconditional support and love, guiding you on your path to healing, spiritual growth and the realization of your deepest purposes.

To conclude this chapter, I leave you with this list of the 100 most commonly invoked angels, and a brief description of their attributes and qualities. You can choose from them, or you can also research others on your own, through books or the internet. There is an infinite number of angels willing to help us.

1. Archangel Michael: Protection, strength and guidance in difficult moments.

2. Archangel Gabriel: Divine messenger, revelation and inspiration.

3. Archangel Raphael: Heavenly healer, physical and emotional healing.

4. Archangel Uriel: Wisdom, illumination and knowledge.

5. Archangel Jophiel: Beauty and divine wisdom, elevates consciousness.

6. Archangel Chamuel: Love and relationships, seeks love and peace.
7. Archangel Zadquiel: Forgiveness, compassion and liberation from resentment.
8. Archangel Metatron: Divine Record and spiritual guide.
9. Archangel Raguel: Harmony and divine justice, conflict resolution.
10. Archangel Azrael: Comfort and support in times of loss and transition.
11. Archangel Haniel: Intuition and sensitivity, strengthens psychic abilities.
12. Archangel Sandalphon: He carries prayers to heaven, protector of music.
13. Guardian Angel: Personal protection and guidance from birth.
14. Angel Mitzrael: Justice and balance in life.
15. Angel Verchiel: Patience and tolerance, cultivate inner calm.
16. Angel Hamaliel: Protects animals and nature.
17. Angel Anael: Divine love, passion and creativity.
18. Angel Camael: Justice, courage and protection.
19. Angel Barachiel: Blessing and hope, brings comfort.
20. Angel Cassiel: Comfort in times of affliction and loneliness.
21. Angel Jeremiel: Reviews the life after death, helps in learning.
22. Angel Melchizedek: Peace and spiritual balance.
23. Angel Nathanael: Cleansing and purification of the soul.
24. Angel Pahaliah: Reconciliation and friendship.
25. Angel Sealtiel: Adoration and contemplation.
26. Angel Umabel: Divine will and dream fulfillment.
27. Ángel Vehuiah: Initiative and courage.
28. Angel Yerathel: Wisdom and deep understanding.
29. Angel Zaphkiel: Mercy and compassion.
30. Angel Raziel: Occult knowledge and divine mystery.
31. Angel Ariel: Protect nature and animals, a guide for the care of the environment.
32. Angel Asariel: Guide to understand and overcome difficult and painful situations.
33. Angel Azariel: Helps in moments of confusion and decision making.
34. Angel Barchiel: Artistic Inspiration and Creativity.

35. Angel Cerviel: Guide to Overcome Addictions and Bad Habits.
36. Angel Dahariel: Promotes compassion and generosity.
37. Angel Elemiah: Protection for travelers and inner strength.
38. Angel Phanuel: Grant forgiveness and repentance.
39. Angel Gavreel: Inspiration for dance and the performing arts.
40. Angel Habuhiah: Protection against violence and conflicts.
41. Angel Iofiel: Helps to connect with inner wisdom and spiritual knowledge.
42. Angel Jeliel: Promotes fertility and responsible parenthood.
43. Angel Kafziel: Protects against envy and jealousy.
44. Angel Lahabiel: Guide to develop psychic and spiritual abilities.
45. Angel Mebahiah: Promotes peace and harmony among people.
46. Angel Nanael: Grant patience and perseverance to achieve objectives.
47. Angel Omael: Helps to overcome sadness and depression.
48. Angel Poyel: Provides support in making important decisions.
49. Angel Rachmiel: Helps in emotional healing and forgiveness.
50. Angel Sitael: Protects against adversities and dangers.
51. Angel Tehiru: Promotes gratitude and appreciation for life.
52. Angel Umahel: Guide for developing empathy and understanding.
53. Angel Vevaliah: Protects against violence and mistreatment.
54. Angel Yezalel: Helps to develop patience and tolerance.
55. Angel Zuriel: A Guide to Overcoming Anger and Resentment.
56. Angel Aziel: Encourages honesty and sincerity.
57. Angel Bahariel: Protects against envy and jealousy.
58. Angel Chavakiah: Helps in the development of spiritual and healing abilities.
59. Angel Dadriel: Provides protection and comfort in times of loneliness.
60. Angel Elemiah: A Guide to Cultivating Gratitude and Appreciation.
61. Angel Faniel: Promotes honesty and justice.
62. Angel Gahuel: Protects against negative energies and evil.
63. Angel Hamabiel: Helps to overcome shyness and insecurity.
64. Angel Iahhel: Promotes understanding and respect among people.

65. Angel Jelahiah: A Guide to Developing Confidence and Self-Esteem.
66. Angel Kamaliel: Protects against negative influences and dangers.
67. Angel Lelahel: Promotes joy and happiness.
68. Angel Mahasiah: Helps in the resolution of conflicts and misunderstandings.
69. Angel Nithael: Provides protection during travel and journeys.
70. Angel Oriel: Encourages creativity and inspiration.
71. Angel Peliel: Helps in the development of intuition and wisdom.
72. Angel Rachiel: Protects against negative energies and envy.
73. Angel Saliah: A Guide to Developing Compassion and Empathy.
74. Angel Tehomiel: Provides protection and support in times of crisis.
75. Angel Umabel: Promotes peace and harmony in relations.
76. Angel Vohamiah: Helps in overcoming obstacles and challenges.
77. Angel Yehudiah: Protects against evil influences and temptations.
78. Angel Zehuti: Guide to develop wisdom and intelligence.
79. Angel Abdiel: Encourages loyalty and selfless service.
80. Angel Barbiel: Provides protection against envy and jealousy.
81. Angel Charbiel: Helps in the development of healing and spiritual abilities.
82. Angel Damael: Protects against dangers and accidents.
83. Angel Eiael: Promotes respect and harmony in relationships.
84. Angel Fakiel: Guide to develop intuition and perception.
85. Angel Gabuthelon: Provides protection and comfort in moments of loss.
86. Angel Hakamiah: Encourages patience and perseverance.
87. Angel Iofuel: Helps to overcome sadness and melancholy.
88. Angel Jael: Protects against bad influences and deceptions.
89. Angel Kaliel: A Guide to Developing Gratitude and Appreciation.
90. Angel Leliel: Encourages honesty and sincerity.
91. Angel Mitzrael: Provides protection against negative influences.
92. Angel Nuriel: Helps in the development of spiritual and healing abilities.
93. Angel Omael: Protects against envy and jealousy.
94. Angel Padiel: Guide to develop intuition and wisdom.

95. Angel Rahatiel: Promotes compassion and empathy.

96. Angel Sahariel: Provides protection and support in times of crisis.

97. Angel Taliahad: Helps in overcoming obstacles and challenges.

98. Angel Uziel: Protects against bad influences and temptations.

99. Angel Vehuel: Guide to develop wisdom and intelligence.

100. Angel Yerathel: Encourages loyalty and selfless service.

What can you ask of Angels?

By opening our hearts and minds to the presence of angels, we can experience their unconditional love and support. In this chapter, we will explore how we can ask the angels for help according to our individual needs.

Safety and Security:

Angels are heavenly guardians who offer us protection and security. When we feel vulnerable or face dangerous situations, we can invoke the presence of angels to surround us with their protective shield. In doing so, we can find comfort and reassurance, feeling that we are supported by divine forces on our path.

Wisdom and Clarity:

In times of confusion or uncertainty, angels can illuminate our path with their wisdom. You can ask them for guidance in making important decisions or searching for a deeper purpose in life. By tuning into their presence, you will open yourself to receive intuitive insights and messages that will help you find the clarity and direction you need.

Healing and Wellness:

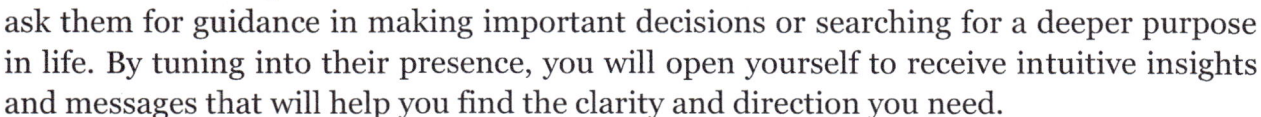

Angels are carriers of healing energy. You can request their intervention to heal on both physical and emotional levels. Through meditation and prayer, you can invite the angels to send their loving healing power to relieve pain and promote health in all aspects of your being.

4. Strength and Courage:

In times of weakness or discouragement, angels can be a source of strength and courage. Ask them to instill in you the courage to overcome challenges and face your fears. With their support, you will find the impetus to move forward on your path and overcome the adversities that cross your path.

5. Love and Relationships:

Angels are full of unconditional love and can help us improve our relationships with others. You can ask them to guide you in healing conflicts, improving communication or attracting positive relationships into your life. By connecting with the loving essence of angels, we can learn to love ourselves and others in a deeper and more meaningful way.

6. Abundance and Prosperity:

If you are looking to attract prosperity and abundance into your life, angels can be powerful allies. You can ask them to guide you to opportunities and solutions that lead to a more prosperous life. By focusing on gratitude and the belief that you deserve to receive abundance, angels can help you manifest your deepest desires.

7. Forgiveness and Liberation:

When we carry emotional burdens and resentments, we can ask for the assistance of angels to free us from the weight of the past. Ask them to help you forgive those who have hurt you, as well as to forgive yourself for past mistakes. In doing so, you will open space for healing and positive transformation in your life.

8. Inspiration and Creativity:

If you are looking for inspiration or need to unlock your creativity, angels can be your guides. You can ask them to assist you in your creative process and reveal ideas and inspiration that flow from deep within you. With their support, you will connect with the universal creative source and allow your talents and abilities to fully manifest.

9. Help for others:

Angels can not only help you, but you can also request their intervention to assist others on their journey. Ask them to send their love and protection to your loved ones, friends or even those suffering in the world. By sending your loving intention, you can become a channel for the well-being and healing of those around you.

10. Spiritual Connection:

Finally, you can ask the angels to help you strengthen your spiritual connection with the divine realm. You can ask them to guide you in your spiritual practice, meditation or prayer to experience a greater closeness with the sacred. By opening yourself to the presence of angels, you can feel a deeper connection to your inner self and your higher purpose in life.

Don't forget that each person has their own personal angel guides, and that they know your deepest needs and desires. Whenever you seek their help, do so with sincerity and trust, knowing that you will be heard and supported in your journey.

Communication with the Angels

Learning to communicate with angels can be a deeply enriching and transformative experience, and in these pages, we will explore how you can open your heart and mind to establish an authentic connection with them.

Understanding the nature of angels:

Before we dive into communicating with angels, it is crucial to understand their nature and purpose in our lives. Angels are spiritual beings from a higher dimension who are always ready to help and guide us on our earthly journey. Communicating with angels requires a receptive and open state of mind and emotion. Here are some practices and tips to help you make this connection:

1. Cultivate inner peace:

Find moments for meditation, reflection and calm in your daily life. Inner peace allows us to tune in to the angelic energy and perceive its messages.

2. Prayer and gratitude:

Expressing prayers of gratitude and requesting the guidance of angels strengthens the bond with them and opens channels of communication.

3. Trust your instincts:

Pay attention to your intuition and the subtle signals you may receive. Angels often communicate through intuitive thoughts, images or feelings.

4. Keep a diary:

Keep a journal to record your experiences, thoughts and dreams related to angels. This will allow you to better understand their messages over time.

5. Creative visualization:

Imagine a bright light enveloping you and connecting you with the angels. You can visualize yourself talking to them, asking for advice or receiving their love and protection.

6. Use crystals and scents:

Certain crystals and scents can help increase vibration and attract angelic presence. Experiment with clear quartz, amethyst and scents such as sandalwood and myrrh, among others.

7. Be patient and responsive:
Communication with angels may not be evident at first. Trust that they are present and working on your behalf, even if you don't perceive them immediately.

Exercise to invoke and communicate with angels:
Now, I will guide you in an exercise to invoke the presence of angels and establish a conscious communication with them. Find a quiet place where you will not be interrupted and sit comfortably with your back straight. Close your eyes and take several deep breaths to relax.

1. Conscious breathing:
Bring your attention to your breathing and take a few deep, slow breaths. Feel yourself filling with positive energy with each inhalation and letting go of any tension with each exhalation.

2. Invocation:
Silently or softly, utter a loving and respectful invocation to invite the angels into your presence. You may say something like, "Dear angels, beings of light and guidance, I invite you with love and gratitude to be with me at this time. May your divine presence envelop me and guide me in this sacred communication."

3. Open your heart:
Imagine your heart expanding like a bright sun of light. Feel love and gratitude within yourself and send this feeling to the angels.

4. Form your question or request:
With humility and sincerity, formulate your question or request to the angels.

5. Listen and observe:
Remain silent for a few minutes and pay attention to any thoughts, feelings or images that arise. Messages from angels can come in unexpected ways.

6. Acknowledgment:
Thank the angels for their presence and guidance. Trust that they have heard your call and will be with you at all times.

7. Conscious return:
Gently open your eyes and gradually return to mindfulness. Make a note of any significant experiences you had during the exercise in your journal.

How to keep a diary of messages from the Angels

The Angel Message Journal is a powerful tool to strengthen our connection with the higher planes. By keeping a record of the signs, synchronicities and messages we receive from the Angels, we can discover patterns, receive guidance and clarity in times of uncertainty and make more conscious decisions aligned with our divine purpose.

This journal also serves as an open door for gratitude and reflection, as it allows us to acknowledge the loving presence of the Angels in our daily lives. In addition, keeping a record of our interactions with the divine helps us to develop a greater sensitivity to these connections, allowing us to cultivate a deeper and more meaningful relationship with angelic beings.

1. Choose a special notebook: Opt for a notebook that attracts and inspires you, whether it's an elegant notebook with decorative covers or a simple planner. The important thing is that it is a sacred place for you and that it encourages you to write with reverence.

2. Establish a daily ritual: Choose a quiet and serene time of the day to write in your Angel message journal. It can be in the morning to set an intention for the day or in the evening to reflect on your experiences. Find a place where you can be at peace with yourself and connect with the divine.

3. Center your mind and heart: Before you start writing, take a few minutes to meditate or breathe consciously. Try to free your mind from negative thoughts and allow the energy of the Angels to envelop you, feeling their love and protection.

4. Dates and times: Record the date and time you received each message or experienced a signal. This will allow you to identify patterns and trends in your connection with the Angels.

5. Type of message or sign: Describe the type of message you received or sign you noticed. It can be an intuition, a vivid dream, a feather found in your path or any other sign that you consider relevant.

6. Context: Write down the circumstances in which you received the message or sign. Were you facing a challenge or making an important decision? Understanding the context will help you better interpret angelic messages.

7. Emotions and sensations: Record how you felt at the moment you received the message or signal. Did you experience calm, joy or peace? Did you feel a chill or a warm sensation? Observing your emotions will give you a greater understanding of the angelic response.

8. Personal interpretation: Write your interpretation of the message or signal received. There are no wrong answers, as personal interpretation is unique to each individual. Over time, you will notice how your perceptions develop and deepen.

The usefulness of keeping a diary of messages from the Angels:

1. Self-awareness and spiritual growth: By keeping a journal, you will gain a greater awareness of yourself and your deepest thoughts. This will help you understand your spiritual path and how the Angels influence it.

2. Learning and guidance: Looking back on your journal will allow you to recognize patterns, lessons and guidance provided by the Angels. This retrospective will give you a greater perspective on your evolution and how to overcome future challenges.

3. Inspiration and comfort: When you feel lost or discouraged, reviewing your journal will remind you that you are never alone and that the Angels are always there to support and guide you.

Preparation for a Reiki session with Angels

In this chapter we will explore the essential preparation for a Reiki session in which we will also invoke the presence and guidance of angels. The connection between Reiki and angels can significantly enhance the healing experience and provide a greater sense of support and protection during the session. We will learn how to attune our energy and open ourselves to receive angelic assistance while channeling the universal life force of Reiki.

Before starting a Reiki session with angels, it is essential to establish a sacred space where the energy can flow freely and the presence of the angels is welcome. Find a quiet, undisturbed place, preferably in nature or in a room where you can feel at peace and harmony. Cleanse the physical and energetic space by lighting incense or purifying candles and consider placing crystals or stones that resonate with angelic energy.

Take a few moments to meditate and relax. You can practice deep breathing techniques to calm your mind and body. Visualize a bright white light surrounding you, creating a protective shield and attracting the presence of angels. Invite your angelic guides to join you in this space of calm and serenity.

Once you feel connected and in harmony, it is time to invoke the angels to accompany you during the Reiki session. You can do this mentally or out loud, expressing your intention with love and respect. Ask your angelic guides to assist you in healing and to guide you towards what is most beneficial for your greater well-being. Remember that angels respect your free will, so feel safe to express your needs and desires.

It is also important to cleanse your own energy. You can do this by visualizing a cascade of white light flowing over you, releasing any accumulated negativity or tension. Another useful technique is "energetic brushing", where you run your hands from head to toe, thus removing any blockages or emotional baggage.

Clearly define your intentions for the Reiki session with angels. Ask your angelic guides what aspects of your life need healing or guidance. You can write these intentions on a piece of paper or simply express them out loud. By doing so, you are opening yourself to receive the wisdom and love of the angels to work on those specific aspects.

It is beneficial to connect with your Higher Self. This deep connection will allow you to receive clearer and more valuable information during the session. You can ask the angels to act as mediators between you and your Higher Self, facilitating communication and understanding of the messages received.

Gratitude is an essential part of any spiritual practice. Before beginning the session, take a moment to thank the angels for their presence and willingness to help you. Also express your gratitude to the universe and the Reiki energy for being available for your healing and spiritual growth. Gratitude opens the heart and strengthens the connection to the spiritual plane.

During the Reiki session with angels, remember to release control and allow the energy to flow freely. Trust that the angels are working with you, guiding you to what you need at that moment. Don't worry about directing the process; instead, surrender to the experience and let the higher intelligence guide the healing.

A complete Reiki Self-Healing Session with Angels

Angels, celestial beings of light and wisdom, are invaluable allies on our path of spiritual growth and emotional healing. Invoking their presence during a Reiki session enhances and amplifies the healing energy, bringing a protective and comforting embrace to your being.

Opening and Protection
Begin the session with a brief prayer or affirmation, expressing your intention to receive healing and open yourself to the assistance of the angels. You can use your own words or a universal prayer, for example:
"With love and gratitude, I open my heart and being to receive the healing of Reiki and the loving guidance of the angels. May this session be a sacred space of transformation and growth. I am surrounded by divine light and protection."
This simple opening establishes a conscious connection with the Reiki energy and the presence of the angels, creating a field of protection and love that will accompany you throughout the session.

Hand Positions
Reiki channels energy through the hands, allowing it to flow where it is needed. Below is a guide to thirteen hand positions for a complete Reiki self-treatment session with angels. Keep in mind that intuition is also important, and you can follow your impulses to modify the positions as you feel necessary.

Position 1: Place your hands over your eyes, allowing the energy to flow into your third eye and release any tension in this area.

Position 2: Place your hands over your ears, healing and balancing the ability to listen and communicate with the world around you.

Position 3: Bring your hands to the back of your head, just above your neck, to release accumulated stress and facilitate mental clarity.

Position 4. Bring your hands to each side of the neck, to relax the muscles in this area specifically.

Position 5: Place one hand on your throat, releasing blockages in expression and communication, and the other on your heart, opening this energy center to love and compassion, both towards yourself and others.

Position 6: Place your hands on your solar plexus, releasing repressed emotions and connecting with your personal power.

Position 7: Place your hands on your abdomen, working on healing and balancing your emotions and relationships.

Position 8: Place your hands on the "bones" of the pelvis, to infuse Reiki energy to your internal organs in the visceral area.

Position 9: Place your hands on your hips, releasing any blockages related to creativity and sexuality.

Position 10: Bring your hands to your waist, to release any tension in the back and allow the flow of vital energy.

Position 11: Place your hands next to your neck for a few moments, to make sure that your muscles are still relaxed.

Position 12: Place your hands on your knees, releasing and balancing the energies of your legs and joints.

Position 13: End the session with your hands on your feet, thanking the angels for their assistance and connecting with the earth to maintain balance.

Invocation of the Angels
In each hand position, invoke the assistance of the angels, requesting their guidance and additional healing. Visualize how the angels surround your body with their wings of light, enveloping you in their unconditional love. You may say:

"Angels of light and wisdom, I invite you to join this Reiki session. Guide my path to healing and harmony. Please help release any blockages and direct the energy to where it is most needed in my being."

Sealing and Acknowledgment

Once you have completed all the hand positions and feel satisfied with the session, close the experience with a prayer of gratitude. Acknowledge the loving presence of the angels and the Reiki energy that has accompanied you in this self-treatment process.

"I deeply thank the angels for their loving presence and the Reiki energy for healing. I feel blessed and at peace with myself. May the light and love I have received expand to the well-being of all beings."

The combination of the healing power of Reiki with the guidance and protection of angels offers you an enriching and transformative self-treatment experience. Remember that this guide is a starting point, and you can adapt it according to your needs and intuition.

Allow yourself to nurture your spiritual path through this sacred union of Reiki and angelology. With each session, you will experience deep inner growth and a greater sense of peace and well-being in your being.

Diagram: positions of the hands in Reiki self-treatment with angels.

A complete Reiki Session with Angels to Heal Others

Establishment of Sacred Space

Once you have done all your individual preparation for the session, and the angels have been invoked, it is important to establish a sacred space for the session. You can do this through a short meditation or prayer, asking for the energy of love and healing to flow freely through you to the patient. Concentrate on opening your Reiki channel and allow the divine energy to flow through your hands.

Patient Positioning

Place the patient comfortably on a stretcher or chair, making sure he/she is relaxed and covered with a blanket if necessary. Explain the process of the session and be sure to obtain their consent before proceeding. Tell them that they will be receiving a combination of Reiki and the loving guidance of angels to facilitate their healing process.

Energy Exploration

Before starting the Reiki treatment, take a few moments to explore the patient's energy. You can do this by placing your hands over their energy field without touching the physical body. Notice any blockages or areas of tension and ask the angels to guide you to the underlying cause of any problems they may perceive. Trust your intuition and allow the angels to lead you in this process.

Reiki treatment with Angels

Once you have explored the patient's energy, begin the Reiki treatment with angels. Place your hands gently a few centimeters over the patient's body in different positions, following the traditional system of Reiki. Connect with the Reiki energy and allow it to flow through you to the patient. Encourage the patient to relax deeply and open to the healing experience.

Hand positions for Reiki treatment of others:

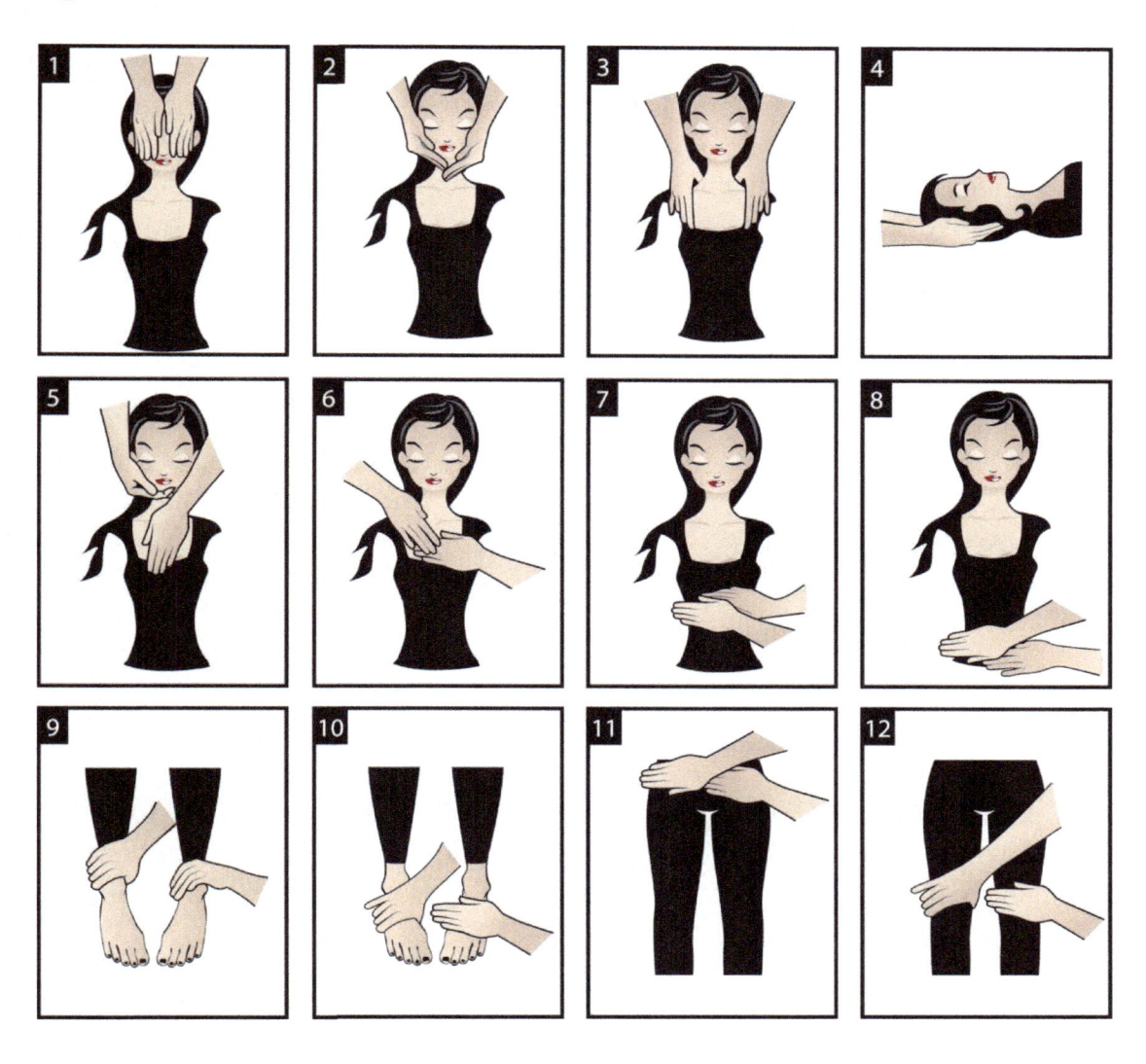

As you perform the treatment, invite the angels to actively participate in the session. You can do this mentally or out loud, whichever feels more comfortable. Ask the angels to guide the Reiki energy to where it is most needed and to help release any blockages or negative patterns that are affecting the patient.

Use of Reiki symbols

During a Reiki session with angels, the incorporation of Reiki symbols can further enhance the experience of healing and connection to the divine. Each symbol is a sacred tool that enhances the practitioner's energy and intention. By invoking the Reiki symbols, the therapist can focus and direct energy more specifically to areas of need for the patient, while the loving guidance of the angels strengthens and supports the process. By tracing the symbols in the air or visualizing them in the mind, the practitioner activates their power and opens a portal for angelic light and love to flow through, creating a profound and transformative healing experience for the patient.

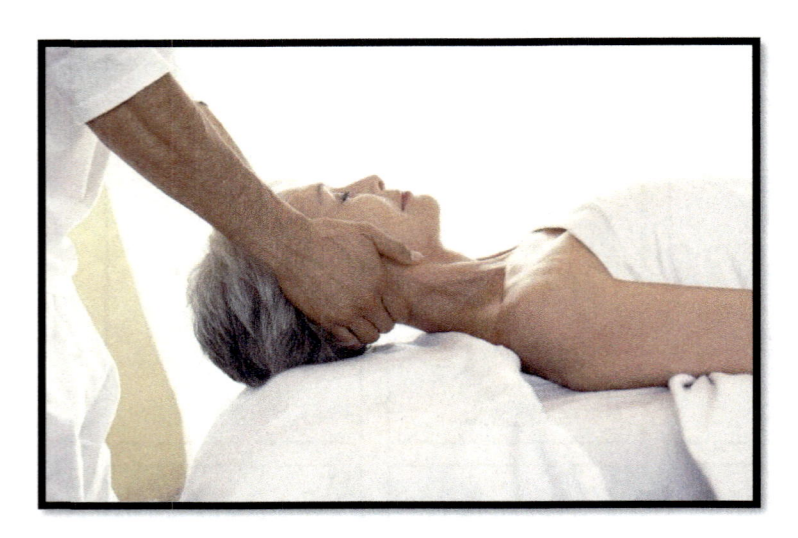

Emotional and Spiritual Healing

As the Reiki energy flows through the patient, blocked emotions or memories may arise. Encourage the patient to allow these feelings to be released without judgment or resistance. Remember that the angels are present to provide love and support during this emotional healing process.

In addition, angels can help raise the patient's spiritual vibration and strengthen their connection to the divine. Encourage them to open their heart and receive the unconditional love that angels offer. Ask the angels to bring messages of inspiration and wisdom to the patient, if appropriate.

End of the Session

Once you feel that the Reiki session with angels has reached its natural conclusion, thank the angels for their assistance and guidance during the session. Also thank the patient for allowing you to be a part of their healing process. If appropriate, share any messages or insights you received during the session.

After the session, it is important that both you and the patient drink plenty of water. Encourage the patient to rest and allow time for integration and reflection after the session.

Remember that each Reiki session with angels will be unique, as each individual has his or her own needs and experiences. As you move forward in your practice, trust your intuition and the guidance of the angels to tailor the session according to what you feel is best for the patient. Always keep your heart open and receptive to the magic and mystery of this beautiful combination of Reiki and Angels.

A complete Reiki Session with Crystals and the Assistance of Angels

In this chapter, we will explore how to combine the healing energies of Reiki, powerful crystals and the loving guidance of angels to perform a complete healing session for another person. This synergy of subtle forces will allow for a profoundly revitalizing and transformative healing experience. The combination of Reiki, crystals and angelic assistance provides us with a powerful tool to balance the physical, emotional, mental and spiritual bodies of the patient.

Before conducting a Reiki session with crystals and the help of angels, it is essential that the therapist and the patient are in a balanced and centered mental and emotional state. Both must be committed to collaborate with the healing process and be open to receive the blessings that the angels and crystals can offer.

Step 1: Prepare the Sacred Space

The therapist should prepare a quiet, clean and sacred space for the session. Light candles and place lovingly and wisely selected crystals to enhance the healing energies. Cleanse the room with incense or incense burners and establish a relaxing and receptive atmosphere.

Step 2: Invoke the Presence of Angels

Before the patient arrives, the therapist can invoke the presence of angels through prayer or meditation. Ask the angels to guide the session and send their healing blessings. Trust that the celestial beings are present to assist in the entire healing process.

Step 3: Patient Reception

Welcomes the patient with warmth and compassion. Listens attentively to their concerns and needs, allowing them to open up emotionally. An atmosphere of openness and trust is essential for healing to flow effectively.

Step 4: Placement of Glass

Before starting the Reiki treatment, carefully choose the crystals that best suit the patient's specific needs. Crystals have different healing properties and can be placed at key points on the body or around the patient's energy field to intensify and focus the Reiki energy.

If you want to formally prepare yourself as a Reiki therapist with Crystals, I recommend you read my book "Reiki with Crystals: complete course of energy healing with crystals, stones and gems" for sale in all Amazon stores. This book is the manual of a course that I have taught for several years, and is accredited by The International Guild of Complementary Therapists, England.

Step 5: Start the Reiki Treatment

Place the patient in a comfortable position, lying down or sitting, and begin the Reiki treatment. Place your hands following the Reiki treatment positions and allow the energy to flow into the patient's body, balancing and purifying their energy centers.

Step 6: Invoking the Assistance of the Angels

Once the flow of Reiki energy has been established, you can specifically invoke the help of the angels to join in the healing process. You can do this mentally or out loud, asking the angels to bring their guidance, protection and love during the session.

Step 7: Emotional Healing with the Help of the Angels

During the session, pay special attention to the patient's emotions. Angels can help release emotional blockages and heal wounds from the past. Remain open to receiving intuitive messages or images that the angels may send to guide the patient's emotional healing.

Step 8: Mental and Spiritual Healing

With the support of the angels, the therapist can work on healing the patient's mind and spirit. You can visualize the healing energy of Reiki and crystals penetrating into the deepest levels of the patient's being, dissolving negative mental patterns and promoting greater clarity and spiritual connection.

Step 9: Closing the Session

Once you feel that the healing process has reached a natural point of closure, thank the angels for their assistance and the crystals for their energetic support. Conclude the Reiki treatment with a sense of gratitude and unconditional love for the patient.

Step 10: Integration and Follow-up

After the session, provide the patient with time to integrate the experience. Encourages reflection and self-care. Offers guidance on how to continue working on personal healing and how to maintain the connection with angels and crystals in their daily lives.

Let us remember that, as therapists, we are simply guides in the patient's healing journey, while the true healing forces come from the divine power and unconditional love of the angels and the universe.

Practice:
How to make a grid of Crystals, Angels and Reiki

In this chapter I will guide you in creating a powerful Crystal Grid with the loving presence of Angels, combining their energy with Reiki to enhance its effectiveness. The combination of these three sacred practices will allow you to open channels of healing and protection, elevating your spiritual connection and empowering your intentions for wellness.

The Crystal Grid is a harmonious arrangement of stones and crystals in a specific pattern that channels and focuses energy toward a particular goal or intention. By incorporating the energy of the Angels, this grid takes on a higher level of celestial vibration and guidance.

Tips for making a Crystal Grid with Angels

In this example we will be focusing on the Archangel Metatron. This angelic being is invoked for wisdom and guidance, as well as protection, as he exists in close proximity to God. There is a sacred geometry design associated with him, which we will be using for the creation of our crystal grid. The design is as follows:

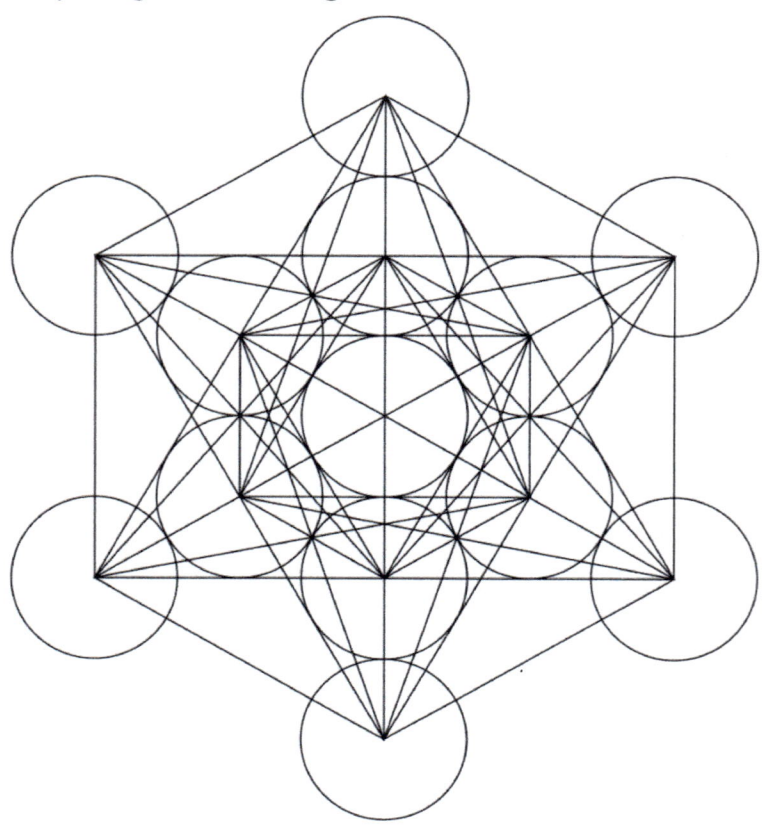

Now, I will explain the process step by step.

1. Preparation and environment: Choose a quiet, serene space where you can concentrate and meditate in peace. Cleanse and purify the space with incense, natural essences or a short meditation to establish a conducive spiritual atmosphere.

2. Crystal selection: Choose stones and crystals that align with the energy and qualities of the angel you wish to work with. Some suggestions are clear quartz for clarity and connection, amethyst for protection and spiritual upliftment, rose quartz for love and compassion, and celestite for communication with the angelic realm. You can also use specific crystals associated with Archangel Metatron, such as fluorite or opal.

3. Intention: Before you begin assembling the grid, clearly state your intention. You can ask for assistance for physical, emotional or spiritual healing, protection from negative energies or divine guidance in a specific area of your life.

4. Personal preparation: Before you start working with crystals, be sure to clear your own energy. You can do a short meditation, a deep breathing exercise or apply Reiki on yourself to balance your chakras and open yourself to the angelic energy.

5. Assembling the Grid: Place a crystal in the center, representing the presence of Archangel Metatron. In my example, I placed a blue opal. Then place additional crystals around the center one, until the geometric pattern is filled. As you do so, visualize the Angels surrounding you with their light and protection. Imagine a sphere of white light encompassing all the crystals, connecting and activating them.

6. With your hands on the crystals, channel the Reiki energy, visualizing the white and golden light flowing from your hands into and through the crystals. You can use Reiki symbols to amplify the energy.

7. Keep the intention clear and visualize how the energy of the Angels unites with the energy of the crystals and Reiki, creating a sphere of loving, healing light that envelops your entire being.

8. Leave the grid in place for at least 21 minutes for the energy to settle and empower your intention. Maximum time the grid should remain in place: until you feel that your intention has been fulfilled. It can be days or weeks.

9. Thank the Angels and Archangel Metatron for their presence and assistance.

Remember that each time you perform this technique, your connection to the angelic realm will be strengthened, and their blessings will flow to you and those around you. May this sacred tool guide you on your path of spiritual growth and help you manifest your highest intentions.

Guided Meditation: Distant Healing with Angels

Welcome to this guided meditation to send Reiki with the guidance of the Angels to a person at a distance. In this sacred moment, we connect with the powerful energy of love and universal healing to bring support and care to those in need. I thank all the Angels and divine beings who accompany us on this journey of compassion and light. Let us begin.

Be sure to find a quiet, comfortable place to sit or lie down. Close your eyes and take a few slow, deep breaths to relax. Feel the air rush into your body, filling you with positive energy, and then exhale any tension or worries.

Visualize a bright white light surrounding you, creating a protective shield of love and kindness. Feel how this light fills you with a warm, comforting energy, giving you strength and peace of mind.

Now, call upon the Angels to accompany you in this meditation. You can ask for the help of your Guardian Angels, Healing Angels or any celestial being you feel close to you. Feel their loving presence envelop you and fill you with peace.

Imagine you are in a sacred and peaceful place, surrounded by lush and serene nature. In this special place, you meet the person to whom you wish to send Reiki and distant healing. Visualize her in front of you, breathing softly and relaxed.

Now, focus your attention on your hands and feel the Reiki energy flowing through them. Imagine that your hands are filled with a bright, healing light, coming from a divine, loving source.

With your hands filled with this healing light, begin to send Reiki to the person in front of you. Imagine how the light spreads out from your hands and surrounds the person with a sphere of golden energy. Feel how this loving, healing energy penetrates every cell of their being, releasing any blockages or pain they may be experiencing.

As you send Reiki, ask for the guidance and assistance of the Angels so that their healing energy combines with yours and magnifies the healing effect. Feel how their loving presence amplifies the energy and directs it to where it is most needed.

Visualize how the person in front of you is illuminated by the golden light and how their body and mind relax deeply. Feel the healing and love flow freely through her, nourishing her being on all levels.

As you continue to send Reiki, feel grateful for the opportunity to share this energy of love and healing with another person. Thank the Angels for their presence and assistance in this meditation.

Stay in this state of sending Reiki with Angels for as long as you wish. You can hold the visualization and healing intention for several minutes or even longer if you feel like it.

When you are ready to end the meditation, say goodbye to the Angels with gratitude for their support and companionship. Thank the person you sent Reiki to for allowing you to be part of their healing process.

Take a few deep, slow breaths, feeling your way back into your present, everyday space. Open your eyes and feel at peace, knowing that you have shared love and healing with another person through this guided meditation with Reiki and the help of the Angels.

May the light and love we have shared during this meditation continue to flow to the person to whom we send Reiki from a distance, nurturing their being and bringing wellness on all levels. You can always return to this sacred space of love and connection whenever you need it. Namaste.

For a recorded version of this guided meditation, you can go to the following website:

https://centerforalternativetherapies.weebly.com/

And look for the section: Guided Meditations

Spiritual protection with the divine help of Angels

The psychic plane refers to our intuitive mind and the ability to perceive beyond the obvious. To obtain psychic protection with the help of angels and Reiki, we can consider the following practices:

Meditation for Mental Clarity: Meditation is a powerful tool for calming the mind and developing greater clarity and focus in our intuition. By taking time to meditate daily, we connect more deeply with our inner wisdom and open the channel to receive guidance from the angels.

Third Eye Reiki Energy Channeling: By focusing Reiki energy on our third eye (the center of intuition), we can strengthen our psychic perception and receive angelic guidance and protection more clearly. Visualizing the energy flowing into this area during a Reiki session can enhance our connection to the spiritual realm.

Energy Protection: Imagining a shield of light in our aura and asking the angels to reinforce it helps us to maintain a protective barrier against negative or unwanted energies. We can visualize how the light envelops us, creating a field of positive energy and repelling any negative influence.

Connection with Guardian Angels: Through meditation and prayer, we can establish a deeper connection with our guardian angels, who are always present to protect and guide us on our journey. By speaking with them in a space of love and gratitude, we open the door to receive their help in all aspects of our lives.

When seeking spiritual protection in the union of angels and Reiki, it is helpful to follow some practical tips that will strengthen our connection with these powerful protective energies:

Daily Practice: Establishing a daily routine for invoking angels and practicing Reiki strengthens our connection and enhances the protective benefits we receive. Consistency and dedication in our spiritual practice opens us to a constant flow of positive energy and divine guidance.

Faith and Trust: Cultivating faith and trust that angels are present and protecting us, even in the most difficult moments, is essential to open ourselves to their help. Believing in their existence and their willingness to help us allows us to receive their blessings and guidance more easily.

Harmonious Environment: Creating a harmonious environment in our home or work space can favor a greater attunement with the energy of angels and Reiki. Using crystals, incense or images of angels can help us maintain a spiritually enriching environment.

Receive Support: Seeking the guidance of a Reiki master or experienced spiritual guide can provide additional support on our path to spiritual protection. Having the knowledge and experience of someone who has walked the path can be valuable to our own spiritual growth and evolution.

Procedure to cleanse your house of negativity, with the help of the Angels

We will explore a powerful and sacred procedure to clear negativity from your home using a combination of the healing energy of Reiki and the loving assistance of angels. Our home is our refuge, a place where we rest and recharge after a long day. However, over time, it is possible for negative energy to accumulate in the space, which can affect our well-being and harmony.

Preparation:
Before you begin, it is essential that you prepare your mind and body for the cleansing process. Find a quiet moment to meditate and connect with your inner self. Breathe deeply and visualize your home filled with light and love. Feel the presence of the angels around you, protecting and guiding you during this process.

Materials needed:
1. Incense or incense burner of your choice.
2. A white candle and a match to light it.
3. A bowl or container with water.
4. Sea salt or coarse salt.
5. A transparent quartz crystal.
6. A white feather.
7. Sandalwood or lavender essential oil (optional).
8. A notebook and pen to record your experiences.

Step 1: Prepare the space
Find a place in your home where you feel comfortable and calm. Place the necessary materials in front of you. Make sure the space is clean and tidy.

Step 2: Lighting the candle and incense
Light the white candle and incense. The candle represents the divine light and the incense will purify the environment, creating an atmosphere conducive to the connection with the angels.

Step 3: Cleaning with salt and water

Take the bowl of water and add a pinch of sea salt or coarse salt. With your hands, dip your fingers in the water and then sprinkle small drops in each corner of the room. Visualize how the water purifies and cleanses the negative energy, bringing it into the light.

Step 4: Summon Angels

Sit comfortably in front of the materials and close your eyes. Connect with your breath and allow your mind to become quiet. Then, out loud or in your mind, give an invocation to the angels:

"Dear angels, beings of light and love, I ask for your assistance in cleansing and purifying this home. May your divine light and unconditional love fill every corner, dissolving all negativity and bringing harmony and peace. Thank you for your presence and guidance during this process."

Step 5: Using the quartz crystal

Take the clear quartz crystal in your hands and program its energy for space cleansing. Imagine how the crystal fills with white light and how its energy expands to cleanse every room in your home.

Step 6: Reiki Healing

With the crystal in one hand and the white feather in the other, begin to walk clockwise through each room. As you go, imagine how the light from the crystal and the white feather clear and release stagnant energy. If you feel a particularly dense area, stop and spend more time clearing that area with love and patience.

Step 7: Gratitude and farewell

Once you have gone through the entire house, return to the place where you started. Thank the angels for their presence and help during this cleansing process. Say goodbye to the ritual with love and gratitude, knowing that your home is now filled with positive energy and harmony.

Cleansing your Aura and Chakra Blockages

The union of angelology and Reiki can provide a powerful and effective method for cleansing and balancing your aura and chakras. The term "aura" refers to the energy field surrounding our body, while "chakras" are energy centers located at various points along our spine. These two aspects of the self are deeply interconnected, and angels can serve as spiritual guides and allies to help us purify and harmonize our inner energies.

The first stage of this process is to establish a connection with the angels, who are spiritual beings full of love and light. Sit comfortably and close your eyes. Breathe deeply and focus on your breath. Visualize a bright white light descending from the sky and enveloping you in its loving energy. You may address the angels in your own words or recite an invocation prayer that you feel comfortable using.

"Exalted beings of light, celestial guardians, I invoke you with humility and gratitude. Help me to purify my aura and release my chakra blockages. I am ready to receive your loving and healing guidance. So be it."

Once you have invoked the angels, focus your attention on your aura. Imagine that you are surrounded by a sphere of bright, white light. With each breath, visualize how that light expands and becomes more intense, eliminating any negative or stagnant energy that may be present in your energy field. Trust the angels to assist you in this process and protect you throughout the cleansing.

If you feel that there are specific areas of your aura that need additional cleansing, you can direct your attention to them and allow the angelic light to work on those specific points. If emotions or situations come to mind that have affected you negatively, do not resist them, simply observe and let the light transform them.

When you feel that your aura is clean and revitalized, it is time to balance your chakras. Begin by focusing on the root chakra, located at the base of your spine. Visualize a bright red light at this point and allow it to expand and spin freely. Feel how this energy connects you to the earth and gives you a solid foundation.

Next, bring your attention up to the sacral chakra, which is located in the lower abdominal area. Imagine an orange light filling this center and releasing any blockages related to your emotions and creativity. Continue ascending to the solar plexus chakra, visualizing a yellow light illuminating and empowering your self-esteem and confidence.

Continue with the heart chakra, located in the center of the chest. Visualize a green light radiating love and compassion for yourself and others. Next, direct your attention to the throat chakra, imagining a blue light that facilitates honest and authentic communication.

Move up to the third eye, in the center of the forehead, and visualize an indigo light that empowers your intuition and inner wisdom. Finally, focus your attention on the crown chakra at the top of your head. Imagine a violet or white light that connects you to the divine and the universe.

Once you have harmonized all your chakras, allow the angels to continue their healing work. Feel their loving presence as they envelop each chakra with their healing light. You can specifically ask them to release any lingering blockages or negative energy patterns that may be affecting your emotional, mental or physical well-being.

Remember that the process of cleansing and harmonizing spiritual energy is not something that is achieved in a single session. It is an ongoing and progressive practice that may require patience and dedication. Feel free to repeat this process as many times as you feel necessary.

Guided meditation to heal emotional wounds with the help of Angels

We will immerse ourselves in a deep guided meditation that will allow us to access the powerful healing energy of the Angels to release and heal our emotional wounds. The combination of angelology and Reiki gives us a unique tool to address our inner world and find healing in every corner of our soul. Before you begin, find a quiet and comfortable place where you can be undisturbed for the duration of this meditation.

Let's begin by taking a relaxed posture, either sitting in a chair with your back straight and your feet flat on the floor, or lying down in a comfortable, receptive position. Gently close your eyes and begin to breathe deeply and consciously. Bring your attention to the ebb and flow of your breath, allowing yourself to relax with each exhalation.

Now visualize a bright, warm light descending from the sky, enveloping you in a blanket of loving protection. This light represents the presence of the Angels, who are here to accompany and guide you in this healing process. Feel their unconditional love surrounding you, providing a safe and sacred space for you to explore your emotional wounds.

Now, bring your attention to your heart. Imagine a glowing sphere of light in the center of your chest, representing your emotional center. Observe this sphere lovingly and allow yourself to feel the emotions that may arise at this moment. Do not resist them; simply observe and accept them without judgment.

In your mind, call upon the Angels to assist you in this healing process. You can say something like, "Dear Angels, I ask you to guide me and help me heal my emotional wounds. May your love and light surround me as I walk this healing path."

Now, visualize the Angels approaching you, surrounding you with their loving presence. You can feel their healing energy flowing into your heart, gently dissolving any blockages or pain you may be carrying. Feel their unconditional love envelop you and fill you with peace.

As you connect with the Angels, begin to remember a specific emotional wound that you need to heal at this time. Don't feel overwhelmed; simply allow the memory to float into your mind calmly and objectively. It may be a past situation that caused you pain, a relationship that hurt you, or a loss that still resonates in your heart.

With the guidance of the Angels, approach that emotional wound and observe how it manifests in your body and emotions. Do not judge yourself for feeling what you feel; remember that this is a safe and loving space to heal.

Ask the Angels to help you release the pain and emotional charge associated with this wound. Imagine their bright light begin to envelop the wound, gently dissolving any negative energy that is stored in it. Feel the Angels' light penetrate each layer of pain and release.

As the wound begins to heal, allow yourself to forgive any person or situation that is involved in this painful experience. Forgiveness does not mean that you are agreeing with what happened, but that you are choosing to release the emotional weight you are carrying. Let the Angels guide you in this act of loving forgiveness.

Now, imagine the sphere of light in your heart becoming even brighter as you heal the emotional wound. Feel your heart fill with love and compassion, not only for yourself, but for others as well. Let this unconditional love expand to every corner of your being, embracing all the parts of you that need healing.

You can ask the Angels to help you replace any negative energy you have released with love and light. Feel their loving energy integrate into your being, strengthening your spirit and raising your vibration.

Remain in this state of connection with the Angels for as long as you need. If you feel there are more emotional wounds you need to heal, repeat this process with the guidance of the Angels.

When you feel the time is right, thank the Angels for their loving presence and assistance in your healing process. Gently open your eyes and carry with you the sense of peace and release you have experienced in this guided meditation.

Remember that this meditation is an act of love and self-care. Allow yourself to return to it whenever you need to and continue to work with the Angels and Reiki to heal your emotional wounds and strengthen your connection to your highest self.

May the Angels be with you every step of the way to deep and meaningful healing.

For a recorded version of this guided meditation, you can go to the following website:

https://centerforalternativetherapies.weebly.com/

And look for the section: Guided Meditations

Guided Meditation with Angels to Manifest the Law of Attraction

This chapter is dedicated to the powerful union of angelology and Reiki to manifest the law of attraction. Here, we will explore a guided meditation that will allow you to connect with the angels and empower your abilities to attract to you all that you desire in your life. This practice combines the wisdom of angels with the healing energy of Reiki to open you to a world of possibilities and create a positive vibration that attracts your deepest desires.

Before you begin, be sure to find a quiet, comfortable space where you will not be interrupted. Sit or lie down in a relaxed position, with your back straight and your hands resting on your legs in a receiving position. Gently close your eyes and take three deep breaths, inhaling through your nose and exhaling through your mouth. Feel how each inhalation fills you with energy and each exhalation releases any tension or worry.

Now, imagine a bright, warm light descending from heaven and enveloping you with its soft glow. This light represents the loving presence of the angels who are with you at this moment. Feel their comforting and wise presence, surrounding you with unconditional love and protection.

As you immerse yourself in this light, you may notice how your body relaxes even more. Feel the healing energy of Reiki flow through you, releasing blockages and balancing your being on all levels. Every cell in your body fills with vitality and harmony, preparing you to work in tune with the angels and the law of attraction.

Now, in your mind, visualize a golden gate opening into a heavenly garden. This garden is a sacred place where you can meet your angelic guides and co-create your deepest desires. Walk toward that gate and step through it with confidence, knowing that you are protected and guided at all times.

As you enter the garden, take in the beauty and serenity that surrounds it. Listen to the gentle murmur of the water and feel the soft breeze caressing your skin. In the distance, you can see a stone bench surrounded by bright flowers. Make your way to that bench and take a seat, feeling the energy of nature envelop you.

At this time, invoke your angelic guides, asking them to manifest and accompany you in this meditation. You can do this out loud or silently, feeling that your heart is open and receptive to their loving presence.

An angel of light appears in front of you, wrapped in a radiant and benevolent energy. This is your guardian angel, who is always by your side, watching over you and protecting you every step of the way. Feel his unconditional love and infinite wisdom as he reaches out to hold your hands.

Together, you and your guardian angel are immersed in a state of deep connection. Feel your energies intertwine and become one, creating a powerful and sacred bond. Trust this bond fully, knowing that your guardian angel knows you intimately and understands your deepest desires.

Now, take a moment to reflect on what you wish to manifest in your life. They may be dreams, goals or intentions that really resonate with your heart and being. Allow yourself to feel the excitement and joy of seeing them already realized, as if they were already here and now.

With this vision clear in your mind and heart, ask your angels to guide you in the manifestation process. Ask them to show you the steps you must take, the opportunities you must take and the lessons you must learn to bring your deepest desires to you.

Listen carefully to any message, image or sensation you may receive from your angelic guides. They may communicate with you in different ways, through thoughts, intuitions or even synchronicities in your daily life. Trust that their messages are always for your highest good and spiritual growth.

As you connect with the wisdom of the angels and their loving guidance, also feel the healing energy of Reiki flow through you, empowering your intentions and raising your vibration. Allow this energy to remind you that you are a limitless being and capable of consciously co-creating your reality.

In this state of deep connection and harmony, repeat silently or aloud your manifestation affirmations. These affirmations are powerful, positive statements that reinforce your intentions and help you align your mind and heart with what you wish to attract.

For example:
- "I am worthy of receiving everything I desire."
- "I attract to me opportunities and people who support me on my path."
- "I open myself to receive the abundance and love that the universe has in store for me."
- "My dreams manifest with ease and in perfect alignment with the greater good."

Repeat these affirmations several times, feeling how their energy expands in your being and in the universe, attracting to you what you desire with love and gratitude.

While you are in this state of deep connection with your angelic guides and the healing energy of Reiki, allow yourself to remain here as long as you wish, knowing that you can always return to this sacred space to receive their guidance and support.

When you feel ready to end this meditation, thank your angels and the universe for the guidance and energy received. Gently open your eyes and return to your physical space with the feeling of being filled with light and love.

Remember that this guided meditation is a powerful tool that you can use whenever you wish to connect with your angelic guides and manifest your deepest desires. Trust that the angels are always by your side, ready to accompany you on your path of spiritual growth and conscious creation.

Allow your heart to be open to the magic and wonders that life has in store for you. Trust that you deserve to receive all the good that the universe has to offer, may the light of the angels guide you and the power of Reiki always accompany you on your journey of manifestation and unconditional love!

For a recorded version of this guided meditation, you can go to the following website:

https://centerforalternativetherapies.weebly.com/

And look for the section: Guided Meditations

How to become a certified Reiki practitioner with Angels

Although the present book will give you all the fundamental information about what Reiki with Angels means and how to use it for self-treatment therapies and also to attend patients, it is preferable that you have previously attended an initial Reiki course. If not, I recommend you to read simultaneously my book "Reiki: Complete Course with the 3 levels, according to the traditional teaching of Dr. Mikao Usui", which is available in the main online bookstores, in its printed and digital formats. This book covers the entire system of Reiki, from beginner, through intermediate to advanced levels. For information on how to purchase it, visit https://www.holosartsproject.com/

Something important to mention is that this book includes the distance attunement for the Reiki Master with Angels level (which you can do once you have learned all the topics of the course), and thus potentiate your energetic levels. The attunement helps your Chakras to open and activate more so you can channel Reiki much better, and the attunement can only be transmitted from teacher to student, so I include that free service with the book.

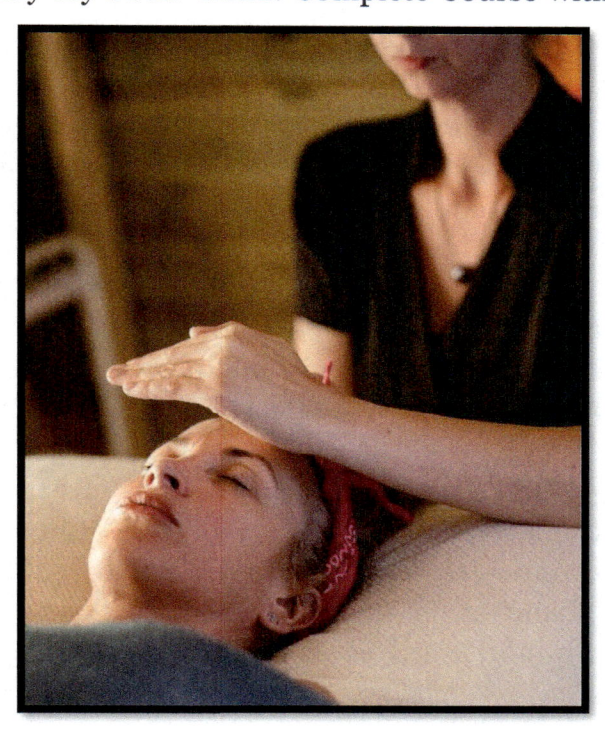

Since this book is also the manual for a full-fledged course, upon completion you will receive a diploma of completion. This course is accredited by "The International Guild of Complementary Therapists" (IGCT), so your diploma will be personalized with your full name, date of completion, my name as instructor, and the IGCT logo. It will be issued by the Center of Alternative Therapies "Sendero Místico", of which I am the general director. To receive it you must write to the email holosartsproject@gmail.com

Preparing for Attunement

Reiki is an energetic healing technique based on the transmission of universal energy through the hands of the therapist to the receiver. In order to practice Reiki, it is necessary to receive an attunement or initiation, which is a process in which the Reiki master opens and activates the student's energetic channels, connecting him/her with the source of Reiki.

The Reiki attunement with Angels is a very special and sacred moment, which marks the beginning of a path of personal and spiritual growth. Therefore, it is important to prepare adequately to receive it, following some recommendations:

- Before the attunement, it is advisable to do a physical and energetic cleansing, avoiding the consumption of alcohol, tobacco, drugs, red meat and processed foods. It is also recommended to drink plenty of water, do moderate exercise and rest well.

- During the attunement, it is important to be relaxed and receptive, with an open mind and a willing heart. You can meditate or pray before the session, asking your spirit guides or the divinity to assist and protect you. You can also wear a white or purple garment or accessory, which are the colors associated with Reiki.

- After attunement, it is normal to experience some physical, emotional and mental changes, such as warm or cold sensations, intense dreams, release of repressed emotions or greater mental clarity. These are signs that Reiki is working on us, cleansing and balancing our energy. To facilitate this process, it is advisable to continue to drink plenty of water, practice self-Reiki every day and keep a journal of our experiences.

- In addition to the above, it is essential to maintain a positive and grateful attitude towards Reiki and towards the master who has attuned us. Reiki is a gift from the universe that helps us to heal and evolve as human beings. Therefore, we should honor and respect it, following the ethical principles of Reiki and sharing its benefits with others.

The Reiki attunement is a unique and unforgettable experience that opens the doors to a new world of possibilities.

Reiki attunement with Angels

Welcome to this Reiki attunement with angels. Before we begin, let me explain the meaning and importance of this powerful practice. The Reiki attunement with angels is a transcendental experience that combines the healing wisdom of Reiki with the loving and protective guidance of angels. Through this meditation, you will embark on a spiritual journey to open yourself to the connection with the celestial realm and allow healing energy to flow through you in harmony with angelic guidance.

To begin this attunement, find a quiet place without distractions. Sit or lie down in a comfortable position, gently close your eyes and bring your attention to your breathing. Breathe deeply, inhaling slowly through your nose and exhaling gently through your mouth. Feel your body relax, letting go of the stress and worries of the day.

Imagine you are in a beautiful garden full of flowers and lush nature. This is a sacred place where the energy of angels is tangibly present. As you walk through the garden, you feel a loving presence around you. The angels surround you with their light and send you a sense of calm and serenity.

See how every flower and tree in the garden is full of life and energy. Feel how the Reiki energy flows through the entire space, filling every corner with its healing light. You feel a deep connection with nature and the essence of everything around you.

At this time, take a moment to set your intention for this Reiki attunement with angels. Close your eyes and place your hands over your heart. Feel your heartbeat and the warmth of your hands. Feel the energy flowing through you.

Mentally or out loud, set your intention to open yourself to the loving presence of the angels during this meditation and in all your future Reiki practices. Ask the angels to guide and assist you in this sacred healing experience. Trust that they are present and ready to give you their unconditional support.

Now, direct your attention to the center of the garden, where a golden light shines brightly. This light represents the healing energy of Reiki, a powerful and loving force that flows through all living beings. Feel how this light draws you to it, beckons you to come closer.

With each step you take towards the golden light, you feel a comforting warmth envelop you. As you get closer, the light intensifies, enveloping you in a warm, comforting sphere. Feel how this sphere of light protects you and embraces you with love.

In the center of this sphere of light, imagine the presence of an angelic being. It may be a specific angel that you feel connected to, or simply a loving and benevolent presence. This angel is here to attune you to the Reiki energy and help you on your healing path.

Observe the beauty and luminosity of the angel. Feel how his presence fills your heart with love and gratitude. The angel smiles lovingly at you and whispers words of encouragement and support. Feel how it fills you with its light and how its presence embraces you with affection. You know that you are connected to the heavenly realm of angels and that their guidance will always be with you.

At this time, the angel gently places her hands on your heart and crown of your head. With each touch, you feel a surge of love and healing energy flowing through you. This energy fills you with a sense of peace and harmony, dissolving any blockages or tensions you may have.

Feel how Reiki energy and angel energy merge into one powerful flow. This unique combination of energies gives you a profound and transformative healing experience. Feel the energy flow through your entire being, from the tips of your fingers to the tips of your toes.

Allow the Reiki energy and the loving guidance of the angels to work together to release any blockages or pain you may be carrying. Feel the healing energy flow to areas of your body that need healing and balancing.

In this moment of deep connection, take a moment to communicate with the angel. You can speak out loud or in your mind, expressing your gratitude for their presence and support in this Reiki attunement with angels. Ask for their guidance and wisdom to accompany you on your path of healing and spiritual growth.

Listen carefully to any message or intuition you may receive from the angel. Trust that your thoughts and feelings are being heard and responded to with love and understanding.

Now, take a moment to receive this healing, allowing the energy to flow through your entire being. Feel the healing energy of Reiki and the loving guidance of the angels intertwine in perfect harmony within you. Visualize how any blockages or negative energy dissolves and transforms into light and love.

Feel how you are filled with a sense of peace and well-being. Feel how this healing nourishes you on all levels of your being: physical, emotional, mental and spiritual. Enjoy this moment of deep connection and feel how you are surrounded by the loving presence of angels.

With gratitude in your heart, thank the angel for her presence and support in this Reiki attunement with angels. Feel the sphere of light gently fade away, leaving you with a sense of wholeness and well-being.

When you feel ready, slowly bring yourself back to the awareness of the space around you. Gently open your eyes and take a moment to thank yourself for this sacred experience of Reiki attunement with angels.

May the healing energy of Reiki and the loving presence of the angels accompany you on your path of healing and spiritual growth. May you find comfort, support and wisdom in the loving presence of the angels as you follow your path of light and transformation. May it be so.

For a recorded version of this guided meditation you can access the following web address, and look in the "Reiki Attunements" area.

https://centerforalternativetherapies.weebly.com/reikiattunements.html

Conclusions

We reached the end of our journey together. It has been a journey full of learning, self-exploration and connection with the universal energy that surrounds us. I hope you have enjoyed every page and have found inspiration and wisdom in these words that come from the heart.

As we close this book, it is time to reflect on all that we have shared. Throughout these pages, I have taken you by the hand through the incredible world of Reiki and the loving presence of angels. Together, we have discovered the healing power of the energy that flows through the universe and how we can use it to transform our lives.

Along the way, I have shared much of my own personal experience with Reiki and the guidance of angels. Each step we have taken has been a wonderful opportunity for growth and evolution. I am grateful to have had the opportunity to share my story with you, and I hope it has inspired you to embrace your own essence and find your path to wholeness.

One of the greatest gifts that Reiki and the guidance of the angels offer us is the possibility to heal our past and free ourselves from the burdens we carry in our hearts. By opening ourselves to the universal energy and the presence of the angels, we allow the light to penetrate the darkest corners of our soul and transform us. In this process, we can let go of the past, forgive ourselves and others, and open ourselves to unconditional love and compassion.

Reiki and the angels also teach us to trust our life path, even when we cannot see clearly what the future holds. Through this powerful connection, we realize that we are not alone, that there is always a loving and compassionate guide with us every step of the way. Learning to trust this guidance allows us to release fear and anxiety, embracing the certainty that we are being supported at all times.

Some people may think that Reiki and angels are abstract or even mystical concepts, but in reality, they are tangible and powerful forces that are available to all of us. Universal energy is present in every atom and molecule of the universe, and angels are beings of light that surround us with love and compassion. We need only tune in to them and allow their positive influence to guide us on the path to wholeness and inner peace.

I encourage you to continue exploring the world of Reiki and angels. This book is just the beginning of an infinite journey towards self-knowledge and connection with universal energy. You can continue to learn, research and practice these wonderful healing and transformational techniques.

In addition, I invite you to continue reading my books and exploring other sources of spiritual wisdom. Each book is a door that opens to new possibilities for growth and expansion. By continuing to read and learn, you will be nourishing your mind and soul, and moving toward a fuller and more meaningful life.

Finally, I want to express my deepest gratitude for having accompanied me on this journey through these pages. It is an honor and a privilege to have shared with you my knowledge and experiences in the world of Reiki and angels. I hope these words have touched your heart in the same way they have touched mine.

Always remember that you have the power to transform your life and that the energy of the universe is there to support you every step of the way. Trust in yourself and in the loving guidance of the angels, and you will see how your life will be filled with light, love and happiness.

Thank you for reading and may the light always be with you on your path!

With love and gratitude, Isis Estrada.

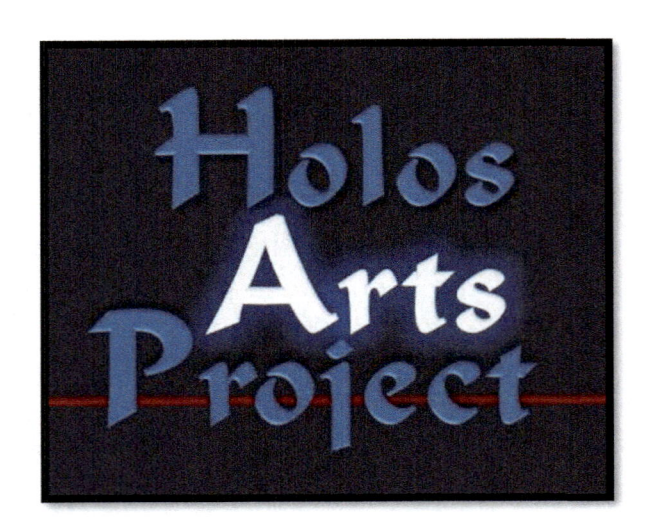

We at Holos Arts Project are grateful for your reading this book. If the content has left you satisfied, you can give us a rating on the Amazon website. We invite you to keep in touch with us, through our website.

Internet pages:
https://www.holosartsproject.com

https://centerforalternativetherapies.weebly.com/

Social Networks
Facebook, official profile: Holos Arts

Facebook, official page: Holos Arts Project

Instagram: HolosArts and CentroSenderoMístico

Youtube: Holos Arts Project

E-mail: holosartsproject@gmail.com

ABOUT THE AUTHOR

ISIS ESTRADA

The therapist Isis Estrada, is a master in psychology, graduated from the University of Minnesota U.S.A. and the University Antonio de Nebrija, Spain. For several decades she has been a professor at several universities in her native Mexico; she is also a best-selling author of diverse books related to alternative therapies and mysticism, and is currently the director of the Center for Alternative Therapies "Sendero Místico" in Mexico City. She is also a member of "The International Guild of Complementary Therapists", London, England.

OTHER BOOKS BY ISIS ESTRADA

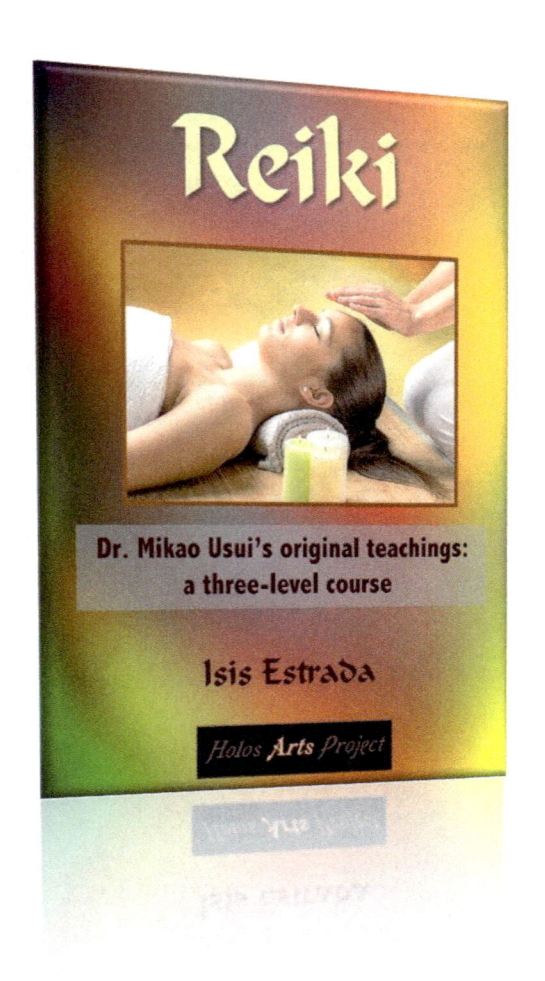

Reiki: Dr. Mikao Usui's original teachings, a three-level course

Complete course that follows the traditional teachings of Dr. Mikao Usui, discoverer of the use of universal energy for healing. The psychologist Isis Estrada, has compiled this manual as a complete course, which includes the attunements and the information of all the Reiki wisdom, beginner, practitioner and master levels.

Buy it on Amazon, in print or digital versions.

https://www.amazon.com/Reiki-original-teachings-three-level-course/dp/B0C9SK1RGR/

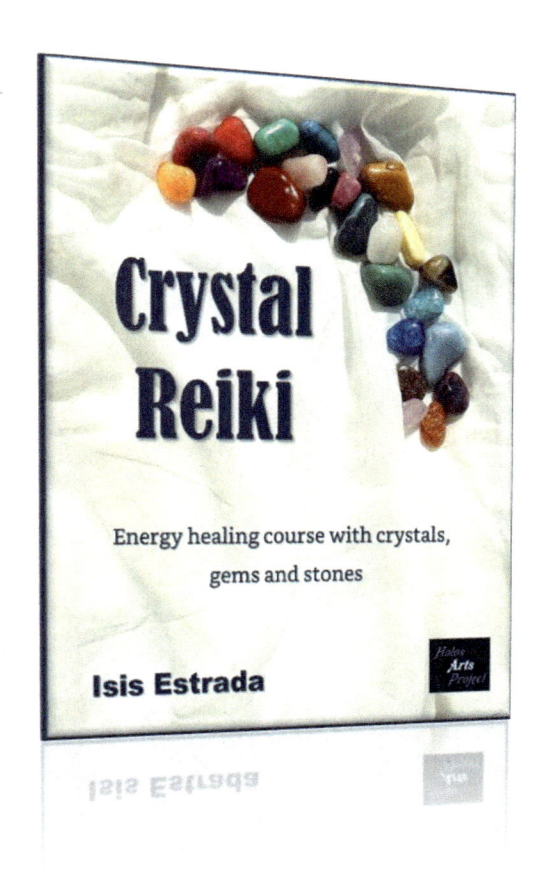

Crystal Reiki:
Energy healing course with crystals, gems and stones

A book that progresses from the basics to advanced techniques in the application of the properties of crystals in Reiki healing sessions. The book includes the attunement as well as an accredited Reiki master diploma.

https://www.amazon.com/Crystal-Reiki-Energy-healing-crystals/dp/B0CCCSTPDV

Animal Reiki:
A complete Course for the Treatment of Animals with Reiki energy

A book dedicated to learn the technique to keep our pets healthy with the universal energy of Reiki. The book includes the attunement, as well as an accredited Reiki master diploma.

https://www.amazon.com/Animal-Reiki-comprehensive-treatment-animals/dp/B0CCXHY1NK/

RECOMMENDED READINGS

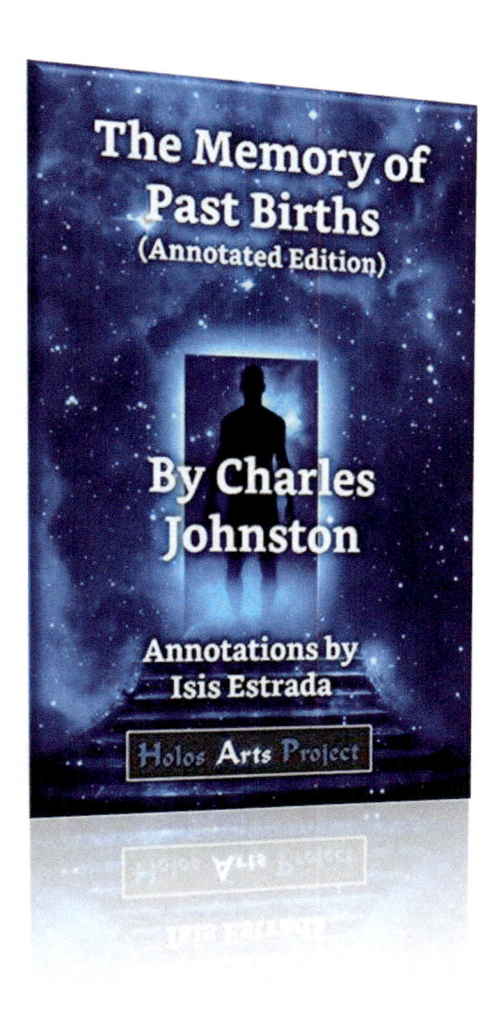

The Memory of Past Births, by Charles Johnston

Do past lives exist? And more importantly: How to remember them? Charles Johnston knew how to bring the millenary knowledge acquired during his travels in the East, and present it in his own time with much accuracy and certainty. Now, it is up to us not to allow his work to be lost, especially when it carries within its letters an inexhaustible source of wisdom for which we are still thirsty. We present, then, the first Spanish translation of *The Memory of Past Births,* which we are sure will become part of your favorite readings on the subject of transmigration, or reincarnation of the soul.

Buy it on Amazon, in print or digital versions.
https://www.amazon.com/dp/B0841FHB28

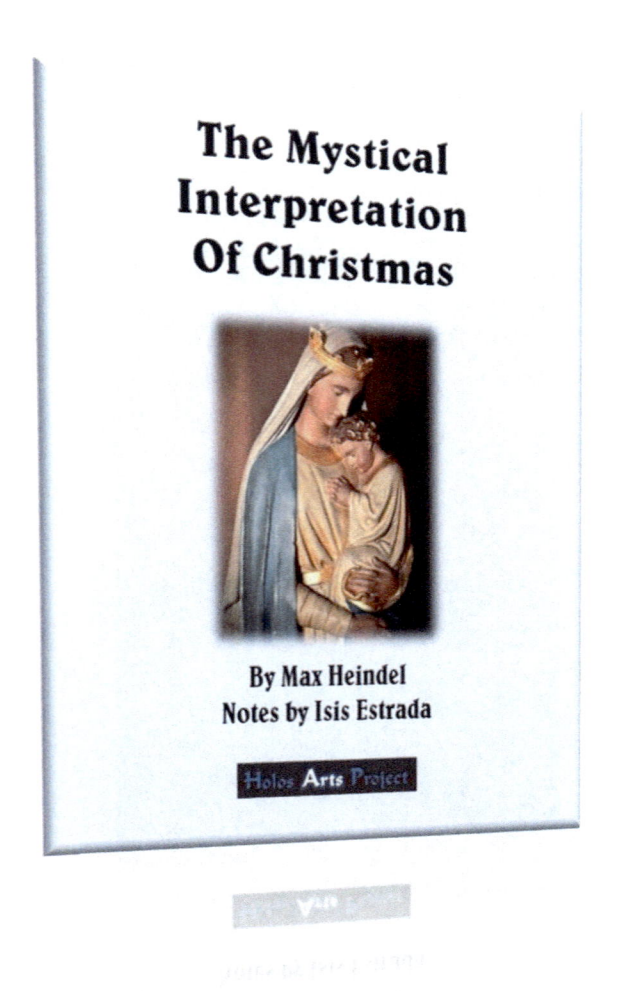

The Mystical Interpretation of Christmas

    Of all the seasons of the year, Christmas season is the one that most rejoices our spirit and predisposes our soul towards the most beautiful virtues. A sense of hope and renewal fills the hearts, and an atmosphere of ethereal happiness permeates our homes.

    Max Heindel, a notable Danish-American mystic, and member of Freemasonry and the Rosicrucian fraternity of his time, presents us with a text that elucidates the spiritual symbolism of Christmas, so as not to forget its deepest aspect in our lives. Buy it on Amazon, in print or digital versions.

https://www.amazon.com/dp/B08P21GT9L

Printed in Great Britain
by Amazon